An Invitation to THE INCREDIBLE JOURNEY OF KNOWING, LOVING, AND FOLLOWING JESUS CHRIST

I dedicate this book
To God who created me, saved me,
and called me into ministry,
To my wife Pam who died from cancer,
To my wife Linda who stands by my side as a loving wife
and partner in ministry,
To our children Jeremy and Sarah who are a blessing from
God and bless me immeasurably it so many ways,
To our grandchildren Nate, Will, and Colman who are a
blessing from God,
To the faithful Christians in Michigan, Kentucky, Indiana,
and Georgia who brought me to faith in Christ, discipled
me in the faith, and those whom I served as their pastor.

William A. Bergstrom

Visit my blog at: knowlovefollowjesus.blogspot.com

The picture on the cover is called "The Road to Emmaus" and was pained in 1877 by Robert Zund. It comes from Luke 24:32 (NAS) which says, "They said to one another, 'Were not our hearts burning within us while He was speaking to us on the road, while He was explaining the scriptures to us?'"

The lyrics of the songs in this book are public domain. Many of the songs in this book, their tunes, live performances, the stories behind them, and their author's history, can be found at websites such as: godtube.com, hymnary.org, YouTube, and others.

The following versions of the Bible are used in this book. The first use of a version is marked by NAS, ESV, or NIV, subsequent references are not identified unless there is a switch to a different version.
- Scripture taken from the NEW AMERICAN STANDARD BIBLE®, (NAS) Copyright © 1960, 1962, 1963, 1971, 1972, 1973, 1975, 1977, 1995 by The Lockman Foundation.
- English Standard Version (ESV) The Holy Bible, English Standard Version. ESV® Text Edition: 2016. Copyright © 2001 by Crossway Bibles, a publishing ministry of Good News Publishers.
- Scripture quotations marked (NIV) are taken from the Holy Bible, New International Version®, NIV®. Copyright © 1973, 1978, 1984, 2011 by Biblica, Inc.™ Used by permission of Zondervan. All rights reserved worldwide.

ISBN 978-1-09833-417-8

An Invitation to
THE INCREDIBLE JOURNEY
OF KNOWING, LOVING, AND FOLLOWING
JESUS CHRIST

Contents

How blessed is the man who does not walk
in the counsel of the wicked,
Nor stand in the path of sinners,
Nor sit in the seat of scoffers!
But his delight is in the law of the Lord,
And in his law he meditates day and night.
He will be like a tree firmly planted
by streams of water,
Which yields its fruit in its season
And its leaf does not wither;
And in whatever he does, he prospers.
Psalm 1:1–3

Oh send out thy light and thy truth; let them lead me, let
them bring me to thy holy hill and to thy dwelling!
Psalm 43:3

Righteousness will go before Him
And will make His footsteps into a way.
Psalm 85:13

For thus says the high and exalted One
Who lives forever, whose name is Holy,
"I dwell on a high and holy place,
And also with the contrite and lowly of spirit
In order to revive the spirit of the lowly
And to revive the heart of the contrite.
Isaiah 57:15

By this we know that we are in Him:
the one who says he abides in Him ought himself to walk
in the same manner as He walked.
1 John 2:5

Preface

Every person's life is a journey which has many mountaintop experiences of joy and wonder, and several valley experiences that bring pain and grief. In all these experiences God is seeking to speak to us. In love he is seeking to draw us to himself that we might receive the greatest blessings there are - to know and love the One who created us and receive all the blessings he has for us now and in eternity. Let me share a few of my mountaintop experiences, and some of my valley experiences, that God used to draw me to him, and that he continues to use to mold me into the person he created me to become.

When I was in elementary school, I liked lying in bed at night, with the window open, hearing the far-off horns of freighters on the river, or the horns of steam engines taking coal to the power plant. Why did I like that far off sound? Was God calling me to him? In the woods surrounding our neighborhood, there was a huge pine tree that stretched above the rest of the trees; a tree that my brother, friends, and I liked to climb almost to the top. When we were close to the top, the view was great! We could see above the rest of the trees, across the river, and into Canada! That beautiful view still comes into my mind. Why? Again, was someone trying to speak to me? Was there more in this world that I could not see?

Today I know that Someone was God. I remember thinking about God and Christianity for the first time during my experience of Confirmation when I was 12. I did not really think about what it meant to be a Christian at that time, but when I was 17, I felt a definite call from God to be a pastor. Being rather shy, I ignored the call and lived a self-centered life; a life that was going downhill into the valley of sin. During this time, God continued to reach out to me while I was in the valley. He mainly reached out to me through a growing desire to understand who he is. He drew me to read books about him, the spiritual life, and the Bible. During this time, in mercy and grace, God even gave me two mountaintop blessings. I meant my wife Pam and about two years later we were married. Then, eighteen months later, our son Jeremy was born. Even before I knew him, God was blessing me and drawing me to him.

1

Preface

When I was 29, I became painfully aware that I really was not saved when I was talking with my pastor who said to me, "Bill, I don't think you're saved!" I listened to him, went home, and read what he suggested. That night I accepted Christ as my Savior. The next day, as I was driving to work, I felt God's presence in me for the first time in my life. Jesus Christ, the Light of the world, had come to *me*! That 'voice' I heard as a child was truly God. This experience was profound and changed my life.

For the next five years, I became involved in spiritual growth and serving in the church. Then, after five years, my wife Pam became ill and, after a nine-month battle with cancer, she went home to be with the Lord. My 7-year-old son and I were left without a wife and mother after her death. We were in a deep valley and missed her greatly. It was an exceedingly difficult experience of grief for both of us. I thank God for his constant presence in our lives, and for a church that was like a wonderful family who helped in many ways through this traumatic event.

Then, two years later, I once again experienced God's call to ministry. The culminating event occurred in 1986 at a camp meeting in Romeo, Michigan. As I sat under a large shade tree on a warm summer afternoon reading Hannah Hurnard's "Hinds' Feet on High Places"., suddenly the world around me seemed to grow dim and I saw Jesus calling me over to Him. As I approached Him, Jesus put His arm around my shoulders and turned me toward an exceptionally large and dark valley with only a few points of light in it. Jesus then said, "I am going to them. Will you go with me?" I instantly said "Yes" knowing that I had just experienced the culmination of my call to serve Christ in full-time ministry.

As I look back at that event, I understand the dark valley to be this world filled with soul's trapped in the deception of their fallen flesh, and the Satanic lies, deception, and allure of this world. Jesus had invited me to be one of those who bring the good news of the salvation that leads to eternal life in paradise. A salvation that is in Christ alone and leads people out of their self-serving lives and are transformed by Christ into citizens of the Kingdom of God.

This was a life-changing event that led to my acceptance of that call, and eventually going to seminary and being ordained in the United Methodist Church. When I was in seminary, God

2

blessed me with a wonderful lady named Linda who became my wife. She and her daughter Sarah, and I and my son Jeremy, went on a journey as a new family and entered ministry one year later. These were wonderful mountaintop experiences.

I have been blessed and thoroughly enjoyed every aspect of my ministry, from Sunday morning services, preaching the Word of God, teaching and discipling others, serving the sacraments, ministering to the sick and dying, officiating at weddings and funerals, ministering to the children, youth, and adults, serving at summer camps, going on mission trips, serving at Emmas Walks, Christmas services, Lent and Easter services, serving in various ways in the community, and much more. There were certainly many mountaintop experiences, and some valley experiences, but my Lord was always with me in all of them.

After 29 years in ministry, I had another journey down into a valley. On a Saturday afternoon, I had a stroke that was serious, and I was on disability for the last two years of my ministry. After a near-death experience, I spent seven weeks in the hospital and almost four years in recovery. Once again, God, my wife, our children, friends, and the church were a blessing that can not be described in words. Their prayers, love, and unending help and support was truly a mountaintop experience for me.

In my retirement, I will continue to serve my Lord Jesus Christ, who has been so kind and good to me through all the mountains and valleys of life. He has never forsaken me, and through all the events of life he has matured me and given me the honor of serving him in his church. He has allowed me to see my son go into ministry and has allowed me to have the privilege of helping others come to know, love, and follow Jesus Christ. In my continuing journey, I will be enjoying my wife, children, grandchildren, family, friends, serving in the church, studying, and meditating on scriptures, leading others to Christ, and reading good books by Christian authors written for the last 2,000 years. I have learned so much about the incredible journey of knowing, loving, and following Jesus Christ since the days of my Confirmation; truths that I know in my mind, and more importantly, deeply within my soul and heart. Truths that I seek to live out daily in my life, and often fail to do so. That means I am still on the lifelong journey of being conformed to the image of Jesus Christ.

Introduction

When I began writing this book, my intent was to have a four-page booklet that the people of my church could use when they were explaining the gospel to people that God led them to. Over the next fifteen years, I kept adding to it to explain more deeply the truth, the depth, and the beauty of the Christian faith. What follows is the result of that intent. It is my desire to share an introduction to the ways God has revealed to us to know him, love him, and follow him, in every area of our lives. My hope is that you will be strengthened in your faith as you read it, or that God will use it to bring you to faith in Christ.

I would like to begin with a quote from the beloved Christmas carol "Away in a Manger" which ends with this phrase, "and fit us for heaven to live with Thee there." Those words are a fitting summary of what this book is about; being fit for heaven by knowing, loving, and following Jesus Christ. A natural question that should come to mind is, "How does God prepare us so that we are fit for living in heaven?"

In the fifteenth century, Thomas à Kempis, a German monk, gave us a succinct answer to this question in the opening paragraph of *The Imitation of Christ* when he wrote,

> *He who follows me can never walk in darkness*, our Lord says. Here are the words of Christ, words of warning; if we want to see our way truly, never a trace of blindness left in our hearts, it is His life, His character, we must take for our model. Clearly, then, we must make it our chief business to train our thoughts upon the life of Jesus Christ.[1]

To seek to know, love, and follow Jesus Christ is to take an astounding journey into a relationship with God that has unknown twists and turns, wonderful surprises and blessings, a transformed life, and some good but often uncomfortable changes and challenges. However, it is a good journey, the journey that God created for us. He invites us to take it, and it always has a good ending: eternity in paradise with the one true God who is good, loving, and kind, with blessings beyond comprehension!

Introduction

You could think of this journey God invites us on as an invitation to enter the greatest story there is - the story of God seeking and calling a people who will respond to him and love him, trust him, and live a life in harmony with him. A life lived in harmony with God means living a life where we grow in our love for God and express this love in service to others. This kind of love is expressed through a growing and deepening sense of joy, peace, patience, kindness, goodness, faithfulness, gentleness, and self-control, as God transforms our hearts, our souls, and our minds.[a]

As Christians, we should not seek to define or understand God on our own; God reveals himself to us. We believe in a God who reveals himself through the Bible, in the person of Jesus Christ, and through the Church, which is the true body of believers in Christ throughout history. It is through these, as the Holy Spirit guides us, that we begin to understand and come to know the true God who created us for himself. What a joy it is to discover that God invites us to go on the journey of entering a deep relationship with him, learning about the unique way we are created to serve him and others, and spending eternity in paradise with him!

Even if you are already a Christian and want to go deeper in your faith, or you want to explore the Christian faith, it is important to understand that Christianity is all about relationships with God and other people. Therefore, you are invited to take several weeks to sit down with someone who is already a Christian and go through this guide together. Then, you will have the added blessing of not only discovering how to know, love, and follow Jesus, you will also be developing a friendship with someone who has been traveling on this journey we all were created for, as declared in the following Scriptures.

"So let us know, let us press on to know the Lord. His going forth is as certain as the dawn; and he will come to us like the rain, like the spring rain watering the earth."[b]

"This is eternal life, that they may know You, the only true

---

[a] See Mark 12:29-31, Galatians 5:22-23
[b] Hosea 6:3 (NAS)

5

God, and Jesus Christ whom You have sent."ª

"but whoever keeps His word, in him the love of God has truly been perfected. By this we know that we are in Him: the one who says he abides in Him ought himself to walk in the same manner as He walked."ᵇ

As you read through this book, you will notice that there are many scriptures included. As Christians, we believe that the Bible is the inspired word of God. Therefore, *always remember that as you study scripture, the primary purpose is not knowledge, which is important, but transformation.* Therefore, ask the Holy Spirit to change you as you study and meditate on scripture.

Also, I would encourage you to write down questions you may want to ask a friend, pastor, or group leader if you are using this book in a group setting.

ª John 17:3
ᵇ John 2:5–6

Chapter 1

The God of Scripture

There is so much to know about God and our journey of knowing, loving, and following him, which makes it difficult to know where to begin, but we must begin somewhere! We will be exploring much about God as we go on our journey but let us begin by looking at the story of creation found at the beginning of the Bible. It reveals how we were created in God's image.

"Then God said, 'Let Us make man *(in Hebrew 'humankind')* in Our image, according to Our likeness; and let them rule over the fish of the sea and over the birds of the sky and over the cattle and over all the earth, and over every creeping thing that creeps on the earth.' God created man in His own image, in the image of God He created him; male *(in Hebrew 'male')* and female *(in Hebrew 'female')* He created them." [a]

Notice that God says, "Let Us make man in Our image". In this verse, God is revealing a profound truth about himself and what it means to be made in his image. God is revealing to us that he is not just one person, but in a mystery we cannot fully understand, is more than one person! Later in the Bible, it becomes clear that God is three persons; the Father, Son, and Holy Spirit; three equal persons, each divine, and yet one God. The Scriptures clearly tell us,

"In the beginning was the Word, and the Word was with God, and the Word was God. He was in the beginning with God. ... And the Word became flesh, and dwelt among us, and we saw His glory, glory as of the only begotten from the Father, full of grace and truth." [b]

---

[a] Genesis 1:26-27
[b] John 1:1-2, 14

7

"Go therefore and make disciples of all the nations, baptizing them in the name of the Father and the Son and the Holy Spirit," [a]

"The grace of the Lord Jesus Christ, and the love of God, and the fellowship of the Holy Spirit, be with you all."[b]

What this means is that the three persons who are one God have such a perfect harmonious relationship of continuous self-giving love to each other that they truly are one God; one sinless, perfect Holy God of perfect love, justice, and righteousness.[c]

One day while directing a camp for upper elementary age children a girl about 10 years old came up to me and asked a question. She wanted me to explain the Trinity! I paused and quietly ask God for a good answer to her question. I then asked her to tell me one word that described God, and she answered, "Love," which was a wonderful answer! I then proceeded to tell her that the Father loves the Son, and the Son loves the Father, and they both love the Holy Spirit. The Holy Spirit loves the Father and the Son. Their love is so pure with each other that in a mystery we can't understand, the three of them are one God. She thought about that for a minute and said, "Now I understand!" It was good she understood because I sure did not!

The mystery, power, love, and purity of one God in three persons is called the Trinity, and is expressed wonderfully in the song by Reginald Herber,

"Holy, Holy, Holy! Lord God Almighty"

Holy, holy, holy, Lord God Almighty!
Early in the morning our song shall rise to Thee.
Holy, holy, holy! Merciful and mighty!
God in three Persons, Blessed Trinity!

Holy, holy, holy! All the saints adore Thee,
Casting down their golden crowns around the glassy sea;
Cherubim and seraphim falling down before Thee,
Which wert, and art, and evermore shall be

---

[a] Matthew 28:19
[b] 2 Corinthians 13:14
[c] see Jeremiah 9:23-24

Holy, holy, holy! Though the darkness hide Thee,
Though the eye of sinful man Thy glory may not see.
Only Thou art holy; There is none beside Thee
Perfect in power, in love and purity.

Holy, holy, holy! Lord God Almighty!
All Thy works shall praise Thy name
in earth, and sky, and sea.
Holy, holy, holy! Merciful and mighty!
God in three Persons, Blessed Trinity.

God, who created us in his image, loves us so much that he is intimately involved in our lives even before we are born! This truth is revealed in these astounding words from King David. [a]

Psalm of David

"O Lord, You have searched me and known me.
You know when I sit down and when I rise up;
You understand my thought from afar.
You scrutinize my path and my lying down,
And are intimately acquainted with all my ways.
Even before there is a word on my tongue,
Behold, O Lord, You know it all.
You have enclosed me behind and before,
And laid Your hand upon me.
Such knowledge is too wonderful for me;
It is too high, I cannot attain to it.
Where can I go from Your Spirit?
Or where can I flee from Your presence?
If I ascend to heaven, You are there;
If I make my bed in Sheol, behold, You are there.
If I take the wings of the dawn,
If I dwell in the remotest part of the sea,
Even there Your hand will lead me,
And Your right hand will lay hold of me.
If I say, "Surely the darkness will overwhelm me,
And the light around me will be night,"
Even the darkness is not dark to You,

---

[a] Psalm 139:1-18

9

And the night is as bright as the day.
Darkness and light are alike to You.
For You formed my inward parts;
you wove me in my mother's womb.
I will give thanks to You,
for I am fearfully and wonderfully made;
wonderful are Your works, and my soul knows it very well.
My frame was not hidden from You, when I was made in secret,
and skillfully wrought in the depths of the earth;
Your eyes have seen my unformed substance;
and in Your book were all written the days
that were ordained for me,
When as yet there was not one of them.
How precious also are Your thoughts to me, O God!
How vast is the sum of them!
If I should count them, they would outnumber the sand.
When I awake, I am still with You."

How does this view of God differ from what you thought before reading this?

Chapter 2

Our Rejection of God

As an expression of the love between the Father, Son, and Holy Spirit, God created humanity *in his image* as the crowning achievement of all creation. The reason God created us *in his image* was to invite us to enter a relationship with him; a relationship of unconditional love between us and God, *and* with each other, as seen in this prayer of Jesus just before his Crucifixion.

> "That they may all be one; even as You, Father, are in Me and I in You, that they also may be in Us, so that the world may believe that You sent Me. The glory which You have given Me I have given to them, that they may be one, just as We are one; I in them and You in Me, that they may be perfected in unity, so that the world may know that You sent Me, and loved them, even as You have loved Me." [a]

Gregory of Nyssa, a church leader in the fourth century, echoed this truth when he said that our destiny is eternal communion with God which reveals itself in endless self-giving relationships of love with God and with each other. In the beginning humanity did live in this kind of relationship with God and with each other. There was no thought of self in the sense of an individual being self-centered. There was a relationship of complete trust and openness between God and humanity, and it existed in a perfect world. However, this relationship of unity did not last long! Please read Genesis three to discover the tragic event that ended the beautiful relationship between God and humanity. ... Make sure you read it!

As revealed to us in chapter three of Genesis, the very first people rejected this relationship of unity and absolute love given to them by God. This was started by the serpent, which is Satan

---

[a] John 17:21-23

11

who asked Eve the very first question that cast doubt about God when he said, "Did God say, 'you shall not eat from any tree in the garden?'" For the first time ever, doubt was planted in the mind of humanity, for it seemed that God had not revealed the whole truth to Adam and Eve, and by extension to all of humanity. This would eventually lead to the same question being asked in multiple ways and forms throughout history.

Dietrich Bonhoeffer[a] said people still ask this question by saying,

> Did God *really* say …? – that is the utterly godless question. … Or does it perhaps not apply to *me* in particular? … This is the question that appears so innocuous but through which evil wins its power in us and through which we become disobedient to God.[2]

The inquiry that the serpent asked was an attack upon the attitude of the creature (humanity) towards the Creator. For the first time, the question of God's integrity was addressed. Rather than saying 'get behind me Satan,' she/he dwelled on the question and humanity caved into the deception. Humanity is deceived by Satan to judge the word of God, rather than simply hearing it, and obeying it, in trust and love.

Eve took the bait and asked Adam to do the same thing, and then the unthinkable happened! They did what God, the one who created them in love, and therefore knew what was best for them, commanded then not to do; they ate the fruit of the tree of knowledge of good and evil.

After Adam and Eve's rejection of God, he came to them and said, "Where are you?" When God said this, he meant something like, w"I have always been one with you in a relationship of complete trust and openness; we walked as one. What has happened?" Of course, God knew what had taken place. Adam and Eve had rebelled against God and rejected him and his way of living. They had fallen out of harmony with him. And in rejecting God, they rejected his love, presence, protection, and guidance in their lives now, and for eternity. This rejection of God is idolatry:

---

[a] Dietrich Bonhoeffer was a German pastor, theologian, and anti-Nazi dissident in WW II, and was hung by the Nazi Gestapo just before the war ended.

a worshipping of someone or something other than God as their god.

Christians call this event The Fall: Humanity's rebellion against God and living in peaceful harmony and communion with him, as they trusted and loved him, and obeyed his commands. God said they would die if they turned from him, and they did; they died spiritually in their communion with God and terribly distorted their communion with each other. It was a rejection that resulted in a world in rebellion against its Creator.

What were the results of the Fall? Instead of a world living in peace and harmony, characterized by self-giving love, we have a world marked by self-centeredness which results in deep patterns of sin and evil. Often, as a pastor, I have seen the effects of people using others to gain something for themselves. The results include broken marriages, broken families, people trapped in cycles of addiction, revenge, violence, grabs for wealth and power, a war-torn world, and much more. In addition to the sin and evil we see around us, the Fall also means that this broken communion with God is for eternity, resulting in eternal separation from him.

The reason the Fall has affected all of us is revealed in the following verse:

> "Therefore, just as through one man sin entered into the world, and death through sin, and so death spread to all men, because all sinned."[a]

Each of us is born with what is called a 'sin nature' because of the Fall. Our sin nature results in a 'war' within us between our self-centered desires to reject God and live according to our own 'wisdom,' and the call God has on our lives to live in a loving and obedient relationship with him. This war is explained in the Bible this way,

> "I know that nothing good lives in me, that is, in my sinful nature. For I have the desire to do what is good, but I cannot carry it out. For what I do is not the good I want to do; no, the evil I do not want to do—this I keep on doing. Now if I do what I do not want to do, it is no longer I who do it, but it

---

[a] Romans 5:12

13

is sin living in me that does it."[a]

This war does not mean that there are two 'forces' within us, but that we have a divided will, that causes inner turmoil which results in sin, leading to separation from God and brokenness in our lives and relationships. It is possible to overcome the effects of the Fall and have a relationship with God and life-giving relationships with others because Jesus Christ said,

> "I have come that they may have life, and that they may have it more abundantly."[b]

The word 'life' in this verse means spiritual life, which is a relationship with God that includes: the receiving of his forgiveness, assurance of eternal life with God, and the presence and guidance of the Holy Spirit. As we learn to be guided by the Holy Spirit, God will give us the power to overcome our sin nature, and develop deep, meaningful relationships with others. This relationship with God however is not automatic. Therefore, it is vital to know how to have it!

People have tried in many ways to have a relationship with God; to bridge the separation between themselves and God. They may seek to do this by assuming that good works, religion, philosophy, morality, etc. (what we *do or believe*) earns us favor with God and eternal life. Some believe that God gave us the Ten Commandments and other laws to help us know how to please him and be allowed into heaven.

However, *God's purpose in giving us his commands was not so we can obey them and therefore earn his favor.* The commandments of God were given to all of us so that we would understand God's expectations of us and come to the realization that all people are helpless to meet them. When we realize how helpless we are to obey all God's commands, there are two choices available to us; either give up and lead self-centered life's without eternal hope, or seek God's solution to our inability to please him through our own efforts.

When some people realize performance does not work, they give up on God and try to heal the brokenness in their lives

---

[a] Romans 7:18-20 (NIV)
[b] John 10:10 (ESV)

through things such as: drugs, entertainment, possessions, power, sex, wealth, family, work, service, alcohol, etc. Again, the Bible makes it clear that none of this works when it says,

"There is a way that seems right to a man, but in the end it leads to death (spiritual death)."[a]

"But your iniquities have separated you from your God; your sins have hidden His face from you, so that he will not hear."[b]

Another way to begin to understand the Fall is with one word; 'pride.' Pride has been known as the essence of sin throughout human history. It is the source of all other sins. Pride is a refusal to trust in, depend on, and submit to God's reign in our lives, and instead to seek to raise ourselves above God and rule our own lives. In his book "Mere Christianity", C. S. Lewis says this about pride, "The Christians are right: it is Pride which has been the chief cause of misery in every nation and every family since the world began."[3]

Pride is the opposite of humility, which is the greatest Christian virtue. In Matthew Jesus begins his teaching known as "The Sermon on the Mount" by declaring,

"Blessed are the poor in spirit, for theirs is the kingdom of heaven."[c]

Jesus is clearly revealing to us that the greatest blessing is to be part of the kingdom of heaven, and the entrance into that kingdom begins with being 'poor in spirit,' or humble.

How to you think pride keeps us from knowing God?

How have you seen the Fall affect you, your family, your friends, and the world?

What have you tried to do to make yourself acceptable to God and have a personal relationship with him?

---

[a] Proverbs 14:12 (NAS)
[b] Isaiah 59:2
[c] Matthew 5:3

Chapter 3

With God there is
No Compromise

How can we overcome our pride? There is hope! God has provided the *only* way for us to be forgiven and overcome our sin-nature! We can come into a relationship with him, lovingly serve him, and be welcome into his Kingdom after we die! That is how loving and kind he is! However, God will not compromise who he is to make this possible

GOD IS ...

The Bible reveals that God is loving and kind, filled with grace, mercy, forgiveness, and a deep love for us, and that he does not want anyone to perish. These are just a few verses that express some of the attributes of God.

"but let him who boasts boast about this: that he understands and knows Me, that I am the LORD, who exercises *kindness*, justice and righteousness on earth, for in these I delight,' declares the LORD."[a]

"Your *love*, O LORD, reaches to the heavens, your faithfulness to the skies. Your righteousness is like the mighty mountains, your justice like the great deep. O LORD, you preserve both man and beast. How priceless is your *unfailing love*! Both high and low among men find refuge in the shadow of your wings."[b]

"The LORD, the LORD, the *compassionate* and *gracious* God, slow to anger, *abounding in love* and *faithfulness*, maintaining *love* to thousands,"[c]

---

[a] Jeremiah 9:24
[b] Psalm 36:5-7 (NIV)
[c] Exodus 3:6-7

"But because of his *great love* for us, God, *who is rich in mercy.*" [a]

"The Lord is not slow about His promise, as some count slowness, but is *patient toward you*, not wishing for any to perish but for all to come to repentance."[b]

Because God's love is pure, he truly does love us deeply, despite our sin and rebellion. As a result, God passionately desires that we become his children and spend eternity with him in paradise.

HOWEVER, GOD IS ALSO ...

The Bible also reveals to us that God delights in justice and righteousness, and that he is holy. Holiness means God has set himself apart from sin and evil and will not allow them to exist in his presence, and in wrath will punish all sin. Here are a few verses that expresses God's justice and righteousness.

"but let him who boasts boast about this: that he understands and knows Me, that I am the LORD, who exercises kindness, *justice and righteousness* on earth, for in these I delight,' declares the LORD."[c]

"The LORD reigns, let the earth be glad; let the distant shores rejoice. Clouds and thick darkness surround him; *righteousness and justice are the foundation of his throne.*"[d]

"Who among the gods is like you, O LORD? Who is like you— majestic in *holiness, awesome in glory, working wonders?*"[e]

"Put to death, therefore, whatever belongs to your earthly nature: sexual immorality, impurity, lust, evil desires and greed, which is idolatry. Because of these, the *wrath of God is coming.*"[f]

"Let no one deceive you with empty words, for because of

---

[a] Ephesians 2:4
[b] 2 Peter3:9 (NAS)
[c] Jeremiah 9:24
[d] Psalm 97:1-2 (NIV)
[e] Exodus 15:11
[f] Colossians 3:5-6 (ESV)

such things *God's wrath comes on those who are disobedient.*"[a]

We must understand that God will not compromise who he is: a holy God. Therefore, he must in justice punish sin, and demands that we be perfect if we are to escape his wrath and live in his presence in paradise as seen in these Scriptures.

"Speak to the entire assembly of Israel and say to them: 'Be holy because I, the Lord your God, am holy.'"[b]

"You must be blameless before the Lord your God."[c]

"Since we have these promises, dear friends, let us purify ourselves from everything that contaminates body and spirit, perfecting holiness out of reverence for God."[d]

"Be perfect, therefore, as your heavenly Father is perfect."[e]

Because God is so good, kind, and loving, it is an obvious desire to want to escape his wrath and have a relationship with him now and for eternity. Being aware of God's demand for perfection should cause us to have a healthy fear that cries out like Isaiah did when he saw the awesome grandeur and holiness of God, compared it to himself, and said,

"Woe to me!" I cried. "I am ruined! For I am a man of unclean lips, and I live among a people of unclean lips, and my eyes have seen the King, the Lord Almighty."[f]

Or Peter when he saw the risen Lord,

"But when Simon Peter saw that, he fell down at Jesus' feet, saying, 'Go away from me Lord, I am a sinful man!'"[g]

---

[a] Ephesians 5:6 (NAS)
[b] Leviticus 19:2
[c] Deuteronomy 18:13
[d] 2 Corinthians 7:1 (NIV)
[e] Matthew 5:48
[f] Isaiah 6:5 (NAS)
[g] Luke 5:8

WHAT'S THE ANSWER?

I used to think that all I had to do was believe the truth of the Christian faith to be accepted as a child of God; to be saved and go to heaven. I was so wrong! So, I began to look at myself as Isaiah and Peter did in the two verses above and understood that belief alone was not enough. This was a huge eye opener!

What more could I do? It certainly seemed, in my eyes, to present a dilemma to God. If I, if all of us, cannot earn our way into a relationship with God simply by believing than what needs to happen? In other words, how can he be a just God who punishes our sins (which would mean eternal separation from God), and at the same time in mercy extend to us the grace and forgiveness that leads to a personal relationship with him, and eternal life in paradise?

How do we begin to understand, and overcome, the lie we bought into when Satan said to Adam and Eve, and continues to say, "Did God say, 'you shall not eat from any tree in the garden'?" As Bonhoeffer said above, it is the same as saying, "Did God really say this to *me*?! Or does it perhaps not apply to *me* in particular?"[4]

We have all fallen into the same trap as Adam and Eve did, and therefore, as Romans 3:23 says, "for all have sinned and fall short of the glory of God," How can we turn back to God? How can we learn to trust God, love him, and obey him? How should we live our lives in a way that God desires us to live? A clue is found in Isaiah[a] which says,

> "For thus says the high and lofty One who inhabits eternity, whose name is Holy: 'I dwell in the high and holy place, and also with him who is of a contrite and humble spirit, to revive the spirit of the humble, and to revive the heart of the contrite.'"

Who is the one who can revive our spirits and our hearts? These questions are what I want to begin to explore in the rest of this book. What follows reveals that there is hope! There is an answer!

---

[a] Isaiah 57:15

Chapter 4

The Only Path to the True God

Throughout scripture God has been reaching out in love and offering people, including you and me, the opportunity to turn to him and step onto the only path of life he had created for us. In a multitude of ways throughout history God has been reaching out to all of us. He offered the path to Adam and Eve[a] and they rejected it[b]. For the first time in Genesis[c] God gave a promise and a foreshadowing of the one who would break the curse of the Fall. He offered the path to the world through Noah[d] and the world rejected it. At that time God used the Ark as a foreshadowing of the one who would open the door and provide us the path to paradise.

Then, there is the major true story of the Old Testament of God presenting to the world the only path to paradise, a story that begins in Exodus and continues throughout the Bible. In Exodus[e] we see God offering the path to the people of Israel through Moses so they could escape slavery in Egypt, as they followed Moses God would guide them to the Promised Land. Then, God gave instructions to Joshua and the Israelites to,

> "Prepare provisions for yourselves, for within three days you are to cross this Jordan, to go in to possess the land which the Lord your God is giving you, to possess it."[f]

---

[a] Genesis 2:15-17
[b] Genesis 3:1-19
[c] Genesis 3:15
[d] Genesis 6:13-22
[e] Exodus 2:24-3:10
[f] See Joshua 1:1-18 which begins the exciting journey of Israel going into the Promised Land.

All these verses, and others throughout the Old Testament, were a foreshadowing of the ultimate event in all of history! The event that opened the door to the one path to the true God, planned by him since before the beginning of time: the birth, the life, the Crucifixion, Resurrection, and Ascension of his Son Jesus Christ!
The answer to the question we asked at the end of the previous chapter is found in a person; and that person is Jesus Christ!

John the Baptist spoke about Jesus when he said, "Behold, the Lamb of God who takes away the sin of the world!' ... Again, the next day John was standing with two of his disciples, and he looked at Jesus as he walked, and said, 'Behold, the Lamb of God!'[a] The two disciples *heard him speak*, and they *followed Jesus*".[b] When Jesus was talking to his disciples one day, he told them, "I am the way, and the truth, and the life, no one comes to the Father but through Me."[c] Jesus is the answer to all the questions we have about what it means to live a meaningful life; the life we were created by God to live!

To enter a personal relationship with God, receive his forgiveness, and receive the gift of eternal life with him in paradise, we must know and believe the following:

- Who is Jesus? What Did He Do?
- The Historical Reality of Jesus' Life, Death, Resurrection, and Ascension

And, in the next chapter we will explore:

- What Jesus, God's Most Precious Son, Offers Us
- How to Receive What Jesus Offers
- The Assurance of Salvation
- Baptized into God's Kingdom

---

[a] The title 'Lamb of God' refers to Jesus being the promised Messiah God would send into the wold to save all who trusted in him for salvation. Jesus is referred to as the Lamb in these God revealed verses: Isaiah 53:1-12, John 1:29-37, Act 8:32, 1 Peter 1:19, Revelation 5:6.
[b] John 1:29, 35–37
[c] John 14:6

Who is Jesus? What Did He Do?

FIRST, JESUS CHRIST IS GOD

Through the Bible God has revealed to us the truth that Jesus Christ is God as seen in these verses:

"In the beginning was the Word, and the Word was with God, and the Word was God. He was in the beginning with God. All things came into being through Him, and apart from Him nothing came into being that has come into being. In Him was life, and the life was the Light of men. The Light shines in the darkness, and the darkness did not comprehend it. ... And the Word became flesh, and dwelt among us, and we saw His glory, glory as of the only begotten from the Father, full of grace and truth."[a]

"Jesus said to him, 'Have I been so long with you, and yet you have not come to know Me, Philip? He who has seen Me has seen the Father; how can you say, 'Show us the Father'? Do you not believe that I am in the Father, and the Father is in Me? The words that I say to you I do not speak on My own initiative, but the Father abiding in Me does His works.'"[b]

"I and the Father are one."[c]

"Now when Jesus came into the district of Caesarea Philippi, He was asking His disciples, 'Who do people say that the Son of Man is?'

And they said, 'Some say John the Baptist; and others, Elijah; but still others, Jeremiah, or one of the prophets.'

He said to them, 'But who do you say that I am?'

Simon Peter answered, 'You are the Christ, the Son of the living God.'

And Jesus said to him, 'Blessed are you, Simon Barjona, because flesh and blood did not reveal this to you, but My Father who is in heaven.'"[d]

---

[a] John 1:1-5, 14 (NAS)
[b] John 14:9-10
[c] John 10:30
[d] Matthew 16:13-17

God said to Moses in Exodus, 'I AM WHO I AM,'[a] and Jesus said in the book of John, "I am the bread of life … I am the Light of the world … I am the gate … I am the good shepherd … I am the resurrection and the life … I am the way, and the truth, and the life … I am the vine …" In saying this Jesus is declaring that he is God!

These verses only touch on who Jesus Christ is. We cannot possibly ever fully comprehend who he is, but we certainly must always seek to know more about Christ. In the fourth century a church leader named Ephraim of Syria wrote the following hymn entitled "Blessed Be That Child!". The song explores the person of Jesus Christ, who he is, and what he has done.

"Blessed Be That Child!"
A hymn of praise and worship inspired by the Nativity
by Ephraim Of Syria

"Blessed be that Child, who gladdened Bethlehem today! Blessed be the Babe who made manhood young today! Blessed be the Fruit, who lowered himself to our famished state. Blessed be the Good One, who suddenly enriched our poverty and supplied our needs. Blessed be he whose tender mercies made him condescend to visit our infirmities.

Praise to the Fountain that was sent for our atonement! Praise be to him who rebuked the leprosy, and it ran away, the one whom the fever saw and fled. Praise to the Merciful, who bore our toil. Glory to Your coming, which gave life to the sons of men.

Glory to the Hidden One, whose Son was revealed! Glory to the Living One, whose Son was made to die. Glory to the Great One, whose Son descended and was made small. Glory to the Power who confined His greatness in human form, His unseen nature in human shape. With eye and mind we have beheld Him.

Glory to the Hidden One, who cannot even be touched by the intellect of those who try to pry into the mystery of His nature, but who, by His graciousness, was touched by the

---

[a] Exodus 3:14

hand of man! The divine nature that could not be touched had His hands bound and tied, His feet pierced and lifted up on the cross. Of His own free will he embodied himself for the sake of those who led him to His death.

Glory to the Son of the Good One, whom the sons of the evil one rejected! Glory to the Son of the Righteous One, whom the sons of wickedness crucified. Glory to him who loosed us by being bound for us all. Glory to him who for our sake both gave the pledge and redeemed it. Glory to the Beautiful, who conformed us to His image. Glory to the Fair One, who did not look upon our foulness. Glory to him who sowed His light in the darkness.

Glory to Him, who could never be measured by us! Our heart is too small for Him; yes, our mind is too feeble. He makes foolish our smallness by the riches of His wisdom.

Glory to the hidden Husbandman (a trusted caretaker) of our intellects! His seed fell onto our ground and made our mind rich. His increase came a hundredfold into the treasury of our souls.

Blessed be the Shepherd who became a Lamb for our reconciliation! Blessed be the Branch who became the Cup of our redemption. Blessed be the Tiller, who became wheat so that he might be sown, and a sheaf so that he might be cut down. Blessed be the Architect who became a Tower for our place of safety.

Let us praise him who prevailed and made us alive by His stripes! We praise him who took away the curse by His thorns. We praise him who put death to death by His dying. We praise him who kept silent and justified us. We praise him who rebuked death that had overcome us. We praise him who went to sleep, and chased our deep sleep away.

Glory be to God, who healed weak humanity! Glory be to him who was baptized, and drowned our iniquity in the deep, and choked him who choked us. Blessed be the Physician who healed wounds with a medicine that was not harsh. His Son became a Medicine that showed sinners mercy.

Blessed be he who dwelt in the womb and wrought within it a human nature: a perfect temple that he might dwell in it, a throne that he might be seated in it, a garment that he might be arrayed in it, and a weapon that he might conquer through it!

Blessed be he whom our mouth cannot adequately praise, because His gift is too great for the skill of orators to tell! Nor can our abilities adequately praise His goodness. For praise him as we may, it is too little. But since it is useless to be silent and constrain ourselves, may He, on account of our weakness, excuse the meagerness of such praise as we can sing.

Ocean of Glory, who has no need to have Your glory sung, in Your goodness receive this drop of praise!"

One of Dietrich Bonhoeffer writings was on the incarnation of Jesus as the Son of God and is included in his book *God Is in The Manger.*

God Is in The Manger by Dietrich Bonhoeffer

"'Mighty God' (Isaiah 9:6) is the name of this child. The child in the manger is none other than God himself. .... Kneel down before this miserable manger, before this child of poor people, and repent in faith the stammering words of the prophet: 'Mighty God!' And he will be your God and your might."[5]

The following hymns, and many more, have been sung about the birth of Jesus Christ as the Son of God.

"Come Thou Long Expected Jesus" by Charles Wesley

Come, Thou long expected Jesus born to set Thy people free;
From our fears and sins release us, let us find our rest in Thee.

Israel's strength and consolation, hope of all the earth thou art;
Dear desire of every nation, joy of every longing heart.

Born Thy people to deliver, born a child and yet a King,
Born to reign in us forever, now Thy gracious kingdom bring.

By Thine own eternal Spirit rule in all our hearts alone;
By Thine all sufficient merit, raise us to thy glorious throne.

"Angels from the Realms of Glory" by James Montgomery

Angels, from the realms of glory,
wing your flight o'er all the earth;
ye who sang creation's story,
now proclaim Messiah's birth:
come and worship, come and worship,
worship Christ, the new-born King!

Shepherds, in the fields abiding,
watching o'er your flocks by night,
God on earth is now residing,
yonder shines the infant Light:
come and worship, come and worship,
worship Christ, the new-born King!

Sages, leave your contemplations,
brighter visions beam afar;
seek the great Desire of nations,
ye have seen the Infant's star:
come and worship, come and worship,
worship Christ, the new-born King!

Saints, before the altar bending,
watching long in hope and fear,
suddenly the Lord, descending,
in His temple shall appear:
come and worship, come and worship,
worship Christ, the new-born King!

SECOND, JESUS CHRIST LIVED A PERFECT LIFE FOR US

Most of us will admit that we are not perfect, and that we cannot be perfect. And yet, God demands that if we are to receive eternal life with him, we must be perfect as seen when Jesus says, "Be perfect, therefore, as your heavenly Father is perfect."[a]

Since it is impossible for us to live a perfect life, God, because of his amazing love for us, lived a perfect life for us through the person of Jesus Christ. Throughout his life Jesus lived

---

[a] Matthew 5:48 (NIV)

in perfect obedience to and in harmony with God the Father. Jesus did this because of his love for and trust in the Father, and a desire to please him and complete the work he came to earth for. We see this in the following Scriptures, the first of which takes place just before Jesus was arrested and crucified.

> "Going a little farther, he fell with his face to the ground and prayed, 'My Father, if it is possible, may this cup be taken from me. Yet not as I will, but as you will.'"[a]

> "I have brought you glory on earth by completing the work you gave me to do."[b]

> "For just as through the disobedience of the one man the many were made sinners, so also through the obedience of the one man the many will be made righteous."[c]

> "Therefore Jesus answered and was saying to them, 'Truly, truly, I say to you, the Son can do nothing of Himself, unless it is something He sees the Father doing; for whatever the Father does, these things the Son also does in like manner.'"[d]

And, in the following Scripture is the amazing truth that God transfers the perfect obedience of Christ to us as a gift when we become children of God!

> "And by that will, we have been made holy through the sacrifice of the body of Jesus Christ once for all. ... because by one sacrifice he has made perfect forever those who are being made holy."[e]

Think on this one question: What does 'being made holy' mean?

---

[a] Matthew 26:39
[b] John 17:4
[c] Romans 5:19
[d] John 5:19 (NAS)
[e] Hebrews 10:10, 14 (NIV)

THIRD, JESUS CHRIST'S DEATH ON THE CROSS SATISFIED THE FATHER'S DEMAND FOR JUSTICE

At the end of his life Jesus, according to God's eternal plan, died because of excruciating torture and Crucifixion on the cross. While he was on the cross Jesus cried out, "It is finished,"[a] indicating that he had completed the work his Father sent him to accomplish taking upon himself the wrath of God caused by our sin, therefore paying the penalty for that sin. This utterly amazing event and what it would accomplish is seen in both the Old Testament and the New Testament. Hundreds of years before Jesus' birth the prophet Isaiah wrote,

> "Who has believed our message and to whom has the arm of the LORD been revealed? He grew up before him like a tender shoot, and like a root out of dry ground. He had no beauty or majesty to attract us to him, nothing in his appearance that we should desire him. He was despised and rejected by men, a man of sorrows, and familiar with suffering. Like one from whom men hide their faces he was despised, and we esteemed him not. Surely he took up our infirmities and carried our sorrows, yet we considered him stricken by God, smitten by him, and afflicted. But he was pierced for our transgressions, he was crushed for our iniquities; the punishment that brought us peace was upon him, and by his wounds we are healed. We all, like sheep, have gone astray, each of us has turned to his own way; and the LORD has laid on him the iniquity of us all. He was oppressed and afflicted, yet he did not open his mouth; he was led like a lamb to the slaughter, and as a sheep before her shearers is silent, so he did not open his mouth. By oppression and judgment, he was taken away. And who can speak of his descendants? For he was cut off from the land of the living; for the transgression of my people he was stricken. He was assigned a grave with the wicked, and with the rich in his death, though he had done no violence, nor was any deceit in his mouth. Yet it was the LORD's will to crush him and cause him to suffer, and though the LORD makes his life

---

[a] John 19:30

a guilt offering, he will see his offspring and prolong his days, and the will of the LORD will prosper in his hand. After the suffering of his soul, he will see the light of life and be satisfied; by his knowledge my righteous servant will justify many, and he will bear their iniquities. Therefore, I will give him a portion among the great, and he will divide the spoils with the strong, because he poured out his life unto death, and was numbered with the transgressors. For he bore the sin of many and made intercession for the transgressors.'[a]

Then, in the New Testament the early followers of Jesus wrote the following about what he accomplished on the cross,

"For Christ also died for sins once for all, the righteous for the unrighteous, to bring you to God."[b]

"But God demonstrates his own love for us in this: while we were still sinners, Christ died for us."[c]

"He was delivered over to death for our sins and was raised to life for our justification." [d]

"You see, at just the right time, when we were still powerless, Christ died for the ungodly."[e]

"and live a life of love, just as Christ loved us and gave himself up for us as a fragrant offering and sacrifice to God."[f]

Why did Jesus allow this to be done to himself? He did it out of love to glorify the Father, and to save each of us who receive him from hell, to cleanse our hearts from sin, and to clothe us with the gift of holiness. He endured all the punishment to draw us away from the temptations of the world and the pride within us, and to draw us to heaven to live with him forever!

So much more could be said about what Jesus accomplished on the Cross, but space will not allow it! How amazing that God would do this for us![g] The song, "When I Survey the Wondrous

---

[a] Isaiah 53:1-12
[b] 1 Peter 3:18
[c] Romans 5:8
[d] Romans 4:25
[e] Romans 5:6
[f] Ephesians 5:2
[g] Thomas à Kempis book, "On the Passion of Christ" is a great book.

Cross" by Isaac Watts, talks about the wonder of what Jesus
Christ did for us on the cross.

> When I survey the wondrous cross
> on which the Prince of glory died,
> my richest gain I count but loss,
> and pour contempt on all my pride.
>
> Forbid it, Lord, that I should boast
> save in the death of Christ, my God!
> All the vain things that charm me most,
> I sacrifice them through His blood.
>
> See, from His head, His hands, His feet,
> sorrow and love flow mingled down.
> Did e'er such love and sorrow meet,
> or thorns compose so rich a crown?
>
> Were the whole realm of nature mine,
> that were a present far too small.
> Love so amazing, so divine,
> demands my soul, my life, my all.

FOURTH, JESUS CHRIST ROSE FROM THE GRAVE
CONQUERING DEATH

Then, three days after his Crucifixion Jesus rose from the grave reversing the curse of eternal, spiritual death that humanity brought on itself in the Fall! Through this astounding event, known as the Resurrection, Jesus conquered death making it possible for us to have eternal life with him.

The following Scriptures describe the Resurrection and what is made possible because of it.

"On the first day of the week, very early in the morning, the women took the spices they had prepared and went to the tomb. They found the stone rolled away from the tomb, but when they entered, they did not find the body of the Lord Jesus. While they were wondering about this, suddenly two men in clothes that gleamed like lightning stood beside them. In their fright the women bowed down with their faces to the ground, but the men said to them, "Why do you look for the living among the dead? He is not here; he has risen!

Remember how he told you, while he was still with you in Galilee: 'The Son of Man must be delivered into the hands of sinful men, be crucified and on the third day be raised again.'"[a]

And, because of the Resurrection the power of death is defeated, and we therefore need have no fear of death or what will happen to us after we die, as we see in these amazing Scriptures,

"For this perishable must put on the imperishable, and this mortal must put on immortality. But when this perishable will have put on the imperishable, and this mortal will have put on immortality, then will come about the saying that is written, 'Death is swallowed up in victory, O death, where is your victory? O death, where is your sting?' The sting of death is sin, and the power of sin is the law; but thanks be to God, who gives us the victory through our Lord Jesus Christ."[b]

"Do not let your heart be troubled; believe in God, believe also in Me. In My Father's house are many dwelling places; if it were not so, I would have told you; for I go to prepare a place for you. If I go and prepare a place for you, I will come again and receive you to Myself, that where I am, there you may be also."[c]

Many people have trouble with the fact that Jesus Christ was raised from the dead. First, if Christ is God, as we have said, then why would it be a problem for him, whom the world was created through[d], to be raised from the dead? And secondly, if Jesus has not been raised from the dead then the entire Christian faith is not true; we have been following a lie, as the following verses say.

"Now if Christ is preached, that He has been raised from the dead, how do some among you say that there is no resurrection of the dead? But if there is no resurrection of the dead, not even Christ has been raised; and if Christ has not

---

[a] Luke 24:1-7, also see Matthew 28:1-10, Mark 16:1-13,
   John 20:1-18
[b] 1 Corinthians 15:53-57 (NAS)
[c] John 14:1-3
[d] Colossians 1:15-20

31

been raised, then our preaching is vain, your faith also is vain. Moreover, we are even found to be false witnesses of God, because we testified against God that He raised Christ, whom He did not raise, if in fact the dead are not raised. For if the dead are not raised, not even Christ has been raised; and if Christ has not been raised, your faith is worthless; you are still in your sins. Then those also who have fallen asleep in Christ have perished. If we have hoped in Christ in this life only, we are of all men most to be pitied. But now Christ has been raised from the dead, the first fruits of those who are asleep. For since by a man came death, by a man also came the resurrection of the dead. For as in Adam all die, so also in Christ all will be made alive."[a]

And, we would have no hope of eternal life in heaven, as the following verses testify.

"Blessed be the God and Father of our Lord Jesus Christ, who according to His great mercy has caused us to be born again to a living hope through the resurrection of Jesus Christ from the dead, to obtain an inheritance which is imperishable and undefiled and will not fade away, reserved in heaven for you, who are protected by the power of God through faith for a salvation ready to be revealed in the last time. In this you greatly rejoice, even though now for a little while, if necessary, you have been distressed by various trials, so that the proof of your faith, being more precious than gold which is perishable, even though tested by fire, may be found to result in praise and glory and honor at the revelation of Jesus Christ; and though you have not seen Him, you love Him, and though you do not see Him now, but believe in Him, you greatly rejoice with joy inexpressible and full of glory, obtaining as the outcome of your faith the salvation of your souls."[b]

In the end we must accept the Resurrection by faith, which God will give to anyone who humbly accepts it. Just because we cannot possibly understand it, does not mean it is not true! As he

---

[a] 1 Corinthians 15:12–22
[b] 1 Peter 1:3–9

says in the following verses.

"After eight days His disciples were again inside, and Thomas with them. Jesus came, the doors having been shut, and stood in their midst and said, 'Peace be with you.' Then He said to Thomas, 'Reach here with your finger, and see My hands; and reach here your hand and put it into My side; and do not be unbelieving but believing.' Thomas answered and said to Him, 'My Lord and my God!' Jesus said to him, 'Because you have seen Me, have you believed? Blessed are they who did not see, and yet believed.'"[a]

"Now faith is the assurance of things hoped for, the conviction of things not seen. For by it the men of old gained approval."[b]

The following beloved song declares the truth and the joy of the Resurrection so clearly!

"Christ the Lord Is Risen Today" by Charles Wesley

> Christ the Lord is risen today, Alleluia!
> Earth and heaven in chorus say, Alleluia!
> Raise your joys and triumphs high, Alleluia!
> Sing, ye heavens, and earth reply, Alleluia!
>
> Love's redeeming work is done, Alleluia!
> Fought the fight, the battle won, Alleluia!
> Death in vain forbids him rise, Alleluia!
> Christ has opened paradise, Alleluia!
>
> Lives again our glorious King, Alleluia!
> Where, O death, is now thy sting? Alleluia!
> Once he died our souls to save, Alleluia!
> Where's thy victory, boasting grave? Alleluia!
>
> Soar we now where Christ has led, Alleluia!
> Following our exalted Head, Alleluia!
> Made like him, like him we rise, Alleluia!
> Ours the cross, the grave, the skies, Alleluia!
>
> Hail the Lord of earth and heaven, Alleluia!

---

[a] John 20:26–29
[b] Hebrews 11:1–2

Praise to thee by both be given, Alleluia!
Thee we greet triumphant now, Alleluia!
Hail the Resurrection, thou, Alleluia!
King of glory, soul of bliss, Alleluia!
Everlasting life is this, Alleluia!
Thee to know, thy power to prove, Alleluia!
Thus to sing, and thus to love, Alleluia!

FIFTH, JESUS CHRIST ASCENDED INTO HEAVEN

Forty days after his Resection Jesus was lifted into Heaven as declared in these and other Scriptures.

"And after He had said these things, He was lifted up while they were looking on, and a cloud received Him out of their sight."[a]

"For Christ did not enter a holy place made with hands, a mere copy of the true one, but into heaven itself, now to appear in the presence of God for us;"[b]

"Therefore He is able also to save forever those who draw near to God through Him, since He always lives to make intercession for them."[c]

Do you believe that what we have said about Jesus Christ is true?

What questions, thoughts, or feelings do you have about what Christ accomplished on the Cross and in the Resurrection?

What questions, thoughts, or feelings do you have about what Christ is doing for us now after his Ascension into heaven?

---

[a] Acts 1:9
[b] Hebrews 9:24
[c] Hebrews 7:25

THE IDENTITY OF JESUS CHRIST IN HIS OWN WORDS

For a wonderful look at who Jesus is, in his own words, read the following from the book of John where he says,
"I am the bread of life" in John 6:32-51,
"I am the Light of the world" in John 8:12-30,
"I am the gate" in John 10:7-10,
"I am the good shepherded" in John 10:11-14,
"I am the resurrection and the life" in John 11:25-27,
"I am the way, and the truth, and the life" in John 14:1-6, and
"I am the vine" in John 15:1-11.

The Historical Reality of Jesus Life, Death, Resurrection, and Ascension

It is especially important to understand that the life, death, and Resurrection of Jesus were historical events that were part of God's eternal plan; his plan to rescue us from eternal separation from him. These were not arbitrary events, nor are they mythical stories. If they had not taken place, then the message of Christianity has no truth! These were central to a plan devised by God before the world was created, as the following Scriptures testify.

"For He was foreknown before the foundation of the world, but has appeared in these last times for the sake of you"[a]

"Then the King will say to those on His right, "Come, you who are blessed of My Father, inherit the kingdom prepared for you from the foundation of the world."[b]

We see these astounding events foretold in many Old Testament Scriptures such as Isaiah above and the following, among many.

Genesis which speaks of Jesus crushing Satan's power one day in the distant future, "And I will put enmity between you and the woman, and between your seed and her seed; He shall bruise you on the head, and you shall bruise him on the heel."[c]

---

[a] 1 Peter 1:20
[b] Matthew 25:34
[c] Genesis 3:15

This verse reveals to us what God said to Satan after he deceived Adam and Eve. The woman refers to the people of God who are represented by Mary the mother of Jesus. Her 'seed' would be Jesus whom Satan would seek to destroy through the Crucifixion. However, in a wonderful way and plan that Satan could not possibly understand or comprehend, Jesus ended up defeating Satan through his perfect obedience to the Father throughout his life, going to the cross, and rising from the dead in the Resurrection!

The following Psalm speaks of God the Father not abandoning Christ to Sheol (Hell) but raising him up in Resurrection power.

"I have set the LORD continually before me; because he is at my right hand, I will not be shaken. Therefore my heart is glad and my glory rejoices; my flesh also will dwell securely. For You will not abandon my soul to Sheol; nor will You allow Your Holy One to undergo decay."[a]

The following Psalm speaks of Jesus Ascension into heaven after the Resurrection where he once again reigns in power over all creation.

"The LORD says to my Lord: 'Sit at My right hand until I make Your enemies a footstool for Your feet.'"[b]

In this 'conversation' between God the Father and God the Son, we see the Father 'inviting' Jesus after the Crucifixion and Resurrection to rise into heaven and return to his rightful place of authority in heaven.[c]

Then, in the New Testament we see many eyewitness testimonies to the Crucifixion, Resurrection, and Ascension of Jesus Christ. A few are:

"After eight days His disciples were again inside, and Thomas with them. Jesus came, the doors having been shut, and stood in their midst and said, 'Peace be with you.' Then He said to Thomas, 'Reach here with your finger, and see My

---

[a] Psalm 16:8-10
[b] Psalm 110:1
[c] You can read about the Ascension of Christ in Mark 16:19 and Luke 24:51

36

hands; and reach here your hand and put it into My side; and do not be unbelieving but believing.' Thomas answered and said to Him, 'My Lord and my God!' Jesus said to him, 'Because you have seen Me, have you believed? Blessed are they who did not see, and yet believed.'"[a]

"And after He had said these things, He was lifted up while they were looking on, and a cloud received Him out of their sight."[b]

"You killed the author of life, but God raised him from the dead. We are witnesses of this"[c]

"We are witnesses of these things, and so is the Holy Spirit, whom God has given to those who obey Him."[d]

"We are witnesses of everything he did in the country of the Jews and in Jerusalem. They killed him by hanging him on a tree, but God raised him from the dead on the third day and caused him to be see. He was not seen by all the people, but by witnesses whom God had already chosen—by us who ate and drank with him after he rose from the dead."[e]

"Now I make known to you, brethren, the gospel which I preached to you, which also you received, in which also you stand, by which also you are saved, if you hold fast the word which I preached to you, unless you believed in vain. For I delivered to you as of first importance what I also received, that Christ died for our sins according to the scriptures, and that He was buried, and that He was raised on the third day according to the scriptures, and that He appeared to Cephas, then to the twelve. After that He appeared to more than five hundred brethren at one time, most of whom remain until now, but some have fallen asleep; then He appeared to James, then to all the apostles; and last of all, as to one untimely born, He appeared to me also."[f]

---

[a] John 20:26–29
[b] Acts 1:9
[c] Acts 3:15
[d] Acts 5:32
[e] Acts 10:39-41 (NIV)
[f] 1 Corinthians 15:1–8 (NAS)

"For we did not follow cleverly devised tales when we made known to you the power and coming of our Lord Jesus Christ, but we were eyewitnesses of His majesty."[a]

True love is revealed when someone chooses to forget self and sacrifice oneself for the one who is loved. That is why the Crucifixion and the Resurrection had to be historical events. They were acts of love! God, through Christ, had to actually go through them to prove his love for us. That is why to doubt that the Bible is the word of God is to give in to a great temptation: to listen to and follow the great liar and deceiver, rather than to love and trust God!

What amazing love! Even before we were created God knew we would reject him. Yet, because of his great love for us, and his desire to have a people who would live in paradise with him, God became one of us in the person of Jesus Christ and went through the Crucifixion. He then rose in Resurrection power proving that true love always conquers evil! And that is not the end of the story! After his Resurrection Jesus Christ rose into heaven, and even today he is at the right hand of God the Father interceding for us![b]

Jesus truly is the One who, "rescued us from the domain of darkness, and transferred us to the kingdom of His beloved Son, in whom we have redemption, the forgiveness of sins. He is the image of the invisible God, the firstborn of all creation. For by Him all things were created, both in the heavens and on earth, visible and invisible, whether thrones or dominions or rulers or authorities—all things have been created through Him and for Him. He is before all things, and in Him all things hold together. He is also head of the body, the church; and He is the beginning, the firstborn from the dead, so that He Himself will come to have first place in everything. For it was the Father's good pleasure for all the fullness to dwell in Him, and through Him to reconcile all things to Himself, having made peace through the blood of His cross; through Him, I say, whether things on earth or

---

[a] 2 Peter 1:16
[b] See Romans 8:34, Hebrews 9:24

things in heaven.[a]

Do you understand why it is important that the birth, life, Crucifixion, Resurrection, and Ascension of Jesus Christ needed to be historical events that fit into God's eternal plan, and had eyewitnesses?

---

[a] Colossians 1:13–20

Chapter 5

Stepping onto the
Path of Following Jesus

In the last chapter we began to explore how we can enter a personal relationship with God, receive his forgiveness, and look forward to the gift of eternal life with him in paradise. We investigated the astounding truth of who Jesus is, what he did for us, and ended the chapter by looking at the historical reality of Jesus's life, death, and Resurrection. In this chapter we will continue our journey as we explore how we can step onto the path of following Jesus by looking at:

- What Jesus, God's Most Precious Son, Offers Us
- How to Receive What Jesus Offers
- The Assurance of Salvation
- Baptized into God's Kingdom

You may have noticed that I have often used words such as 'journey,' 'path' or 'stepping onto' to describe how we can follow Jesus. These words are used often in scripture to provide us with clues about how we can live the life God created us for, as the following Scriptures declare:

"O send out Your light and Your truth, let them lead me; let them bring me to Your holy hill and to Your dwelling places."[a]

"Your word is a lamp to my feet and a light to my path."[b]

"Enter through the narrow gate; for the gate is wide and the way is broad that leads to destruction, and there are many who enter through it. "For the gate is small and the way is narrow that leads to life, and there are few who find it."[c]

---

[a] Psalm 43:3
[b] Psalm 119:105
[c] Matthew 7:13–14

I remember very well, as I shared in the forward, the day that God offered to me the opportunity to change the path I was walking on and step onto the path of following Jesus. I am so thankful that God continues to offer the path to all people today!

What Jesus, God's Most Precious Son, Offers Us

In Jeremiah we hear God saying to Jeremiah, and to us, that we are to "extract the precious from the worthless."[a] The word 'precious' means that which is costly, valuable, prized, rare, splendid, and highly valued. In scripture it is used for the Word of God, stones on the crown of David, stones for the foundation of the temple, God's love and kindness and taking refuge in it. The death of God's people is called precious, as is true understanding. Above all of these, it refers to Christ: he is the Word of God, the cornerstone of the church. He is wisdom and the Sheppard we can take refuge in.

We must extract the 'precious' that is of eternal value which above all is Jesus Christ who is truth, from all the lies and deceptions around us. We must learn to focus on what is truly of God. The preciousness of God is to focus on Christ above all, to love and adore him above all else. He is the Word of God, the precious jewel, the true foundation, our only true refuge in this world. There is no understanding without him. His life, and the life he offers us, is life indeed. There is no other!

The Gospel of Jesus Christ is wonderful news because of what Jesus did on the cross and through his Resurrection. However, it is much more! It is also about what God offers to us individually because of these events. Because these two events took place, God can *offer us* some remarkable gifts. He offers to wipe out the guilt of our sin, to take upon himself the punishment each one of us deserves because of our sins, to give each of us unconditional forgiveness, to give of his presence in our lives through the gift of the Holy Spirit, and to give us the hope of eternal life with him in paradise. All we can do is receive his gift by faith!

When the Bible speaks of 'faith' we can begin to get an

---

[a] Jeremiah 15:19-21

understanding of what it means when we look at Hebrews which says, "Now faith is the assurance of things hoped for, the conviction of things not seen."[a] What follows this verse is a testimony to many men and women throughout the Old Testament who were people of faith. Their stories are wonderful examples of faith and the awesome work God does through them because of their faith! I invite you to take the time to read Hebrews 11, and dwell on what having faith really means!

Now, think about how the truth that God working through faith did not end with the Old Testament! It continues through the New Testament and is true today! There are billions of people throughout history, some of whose stories we know, but most we do not know, who had faith in Jesus Christ and served him well as children of God.

Ultimately, we must accept what God tells us in scripture. Not by using our own wisdom, understanding, or intelligence, but to simply have a deep confidence in the actual existence of God and thus building trust in the evidence God gives us that we cannot possibly grasp by ourselves. It MUST come by faith which is a gift from God himself!

The result of receiving these gifts God offers us is true freedom. Freedom from the guilt of sin. Freedom from the shame of our sin. Freedom from the fear of God's judgment and punishment. Freedom from self-centeredness. Freedom to be the person God created each of us to be. It is wonderful to know that the Holy Spirit is constantly working in us to become all the God created us to be. *For to serve God is perfect freedom!*

How to Receive What Jesus Offers

Believing what has been discussed up to this point does NOT make someone a Christian, a child of God! God does not impose himself on us. He offers himself and what we have learned so far to us. *But, if we are to receive God into our life and what he offers, a response is required.* What is the accepted response?

---

[a] Hebrews 11:1

GOD PURSUES US

Throughout the Bible God tells us that he sends the Holy Spirit to draw us to him and make us aware of our need for salvation. A few verses that reveal this truth are below.

"You send forth Your Spirit, they are created; and You renew the face of the ground."[a]

"Where can I go from Your Spirit? Or where can I flee from Your presence?" [b]

"Now we have received, not the spirit of the world, but the Spirit who is from God, so that we may know the things freely given to us by God,"[c]

One person put it this way, "God is the Hound of Heaven." By this he meant that God, through his Spirit, is seeking to awaken all people to the truth of what the Bible says to us, and of our need for Christ. We call this the *Prevenient Grace* of God, which is God pursuing us and seeking to draw us to him for salvation.

Have you ever felt that God was trying to get your attention?

How did God do it?

---

[a] Psalm 104:30
[b] Psalm 139:7
[c] 1 Corinthians 2:12

43

A CHOICE MUST BE MADE

To enter a saving relationship with God it is important to understand that salvation is a journey and not an event. It is a journey that is initiated when the Spirit of God gives us a desire to believe in, receive, *and* follow Jesus Christ.

The journey begins when we make the choice to believe in and receive Jesus Christ as our Savior, continues as we learn how to follow him, and then allows the Holy Spirit transforms us from a self-centered person into a life-giving person whose life has Jesus at its center, and grows in love for God.

An amazing truth that we discover in the Bible is that God, through the Holy Spirit, makes us aware of the truths we have discussed. Now each person must choose which path they want to take in life: the path that leads to an eternal saving relationship with God through Jesus Christ, or the path that leads to eternal separation from God. Jesus explains this when he says,

> "Enter through the narrow gate. For wide is the gate and broad is the road (journey) that leads to destruction, and many enter through it. But small is the gate and narrow the road (journey) that leads to life and only a few find it."[a]

Because of his great love for us, Jesus is revealing that we have a choice to make and that there are significant, eternal consequences of that choice.

First, Jesus is making it truly clear that, unfortunately, many people make the choice to follow the path that leads to destruction. By using the word 'destruction' Jesus is making it noticeably clear that those who do not believe in him and choose not to humbly receive him into their lives as their Savior and follow him as Lord, will spend eternity in a place of torment called hell. In his book *Exclusion and Embrace* Miroslav Volf makes it clear that God does reach out to everyone with open arms of love, but they resist him:

> "God will judge, not because God gives people what they deserve, but because some people refuse to receive what no one deserves; if evildoers experience God's terror, it will not be because they have done evil, but because they have

---

[a] Matthew 7:13, 14

resisted to the end the powerful lure of the open arms of the crucified Messiah."[6]

It is not pleasant to think or hear about hell, but shouldn't the truth be told so that people can at least make an informed choice?

The other choice offered to us is the opportunity to enter through a small gate that leads to eternal life in paradise. This gate is 'small' because it is the only one available to us and requires humility to go through it. Jesus also makes it clear that we must seek this 'gate' that opens onto the path of eternal life in the Kingdom of God, indicating that it requires that the desire to go through the gate is of vital importance.

If you would like a deeper look at why a choice must be made, you can do a study of Romans chapters 4-8 which are a wonderful revelation from God of what Jesus did for us to free us from sin and open the door to eternal life in paradise.

Which 'path' do you honestly think you are traveling on right now? How do you know?

Are you interested in knowing how to enter through the gate that leads to the path of knowing, loving, and following Jesus Christ?

WE MUST TRUST IN AND RECEIVE JESUS CHRIST

The journey of becoming a child of God begins with a trust in Jesus Christ as Savior and receiving him and the gift of salvation by personal invitation. The following verses represent just a few that extend the invitation God makes to all people.

"Then you will say on that day,
'I will give thanks to You, O Lord;
For although You were angry with me,
Your anger is turned away, and You comfort me.
Behold, God is my salvation,
I will trust and not be afraid;
For the Lord God is my strength and song,
And He has become my salvation.'
Therefore you will joyously draw water
From the springs of salvation.
And in that day you will say,
'Give thanks to the Lord, call on His name.
Make known His deeds among the peoples;
Make them remember that His name is exalted."
Isaiah 12:1–4

The words "draw water from the springs of salvation," are fulfilled in John where Jesus declares that he is the 'springs of salvation' when he says to the women he meets at a well,

"If you knew the gift of God, and who it is who says to you, 'Give Me a drink,' you would have asked Him, and He would have given you living water." And, "Now on the last day, the great day of the feast, Jesus stood and cried out, saying, 'If anyone is thirsty, let Him come to Me and drink. He who believes in Me, as the Scripture said, 'From his innermost being will flow rivers of living water.'"[a]

"But as many as received Him, to them He gave the right to become children of God, even to those who believe in His name,"[b]

"For God so loved the world, that he gave His only begotten

---

[a] John 4:10 and 7:37-38
[b] John 1:12

Son, that whoever believes in Him shall not perish, but have eternal life. For God did not send the Son into the world to judge the world, but that the world might be saved through Him. He who believes in Him is not judged; he who does not believe has been judged already, because he has not believed in the name of the only begotten Son of God. This is the judgment, that the Light has come into the world, and men loved the darkness rather than the Light, for their deeds were evil. For everyone who does evil hates the Light, and does not come to the Light for fear that his deeds will be exposed. But he who practices the truth comes to the Light, so that his deeds may be manifested as having been wrought in God."[a]

"That if you confess with your mouth, 'Jesus is Lord,' and believe in your heart that God raised Him from the dead, you will be saved."[b]

"For it is by grace you have been saved, through faith, and this not from yourselves, it is the gift of God, not by works, so that no one can boast."[c]

"Now faith is the assurance of things hoped for, the conviction of things not seen. ... And without faith it is impossible to please Him, for he who comes to God must believe that He is and that He is a rewarder of those who seek Him."[d]

"Here I am! I stand at the door and knock. If anyone hears my voice and opens the door, I will come in and eat with him, and he with me."[e]

There is a story Jesus told in Luke[f] about two sons who needed to make the decision about being in their father's house (an allegory about humbling ourselves and receiving Jesus Christ as our Savior) or to reject the invitation. The younger son rejected the invitation and instead took his inheritance, left his father's

---

[a] John 3:16–21
[b] Romans 10:9
[c] Ephesians 2:8, 9
[d] Hebrews 11:1, 6 (NAS)
[e] Revelation 3:20
[f] Luke 15:11–32

house, and spent the inheritance foolishly. After living with a farmer and eating pig's food, he wised up, humbled himself and returned to the father's house, hoping to be accepted as a servant. However, when he returned home the ...

> "father saw him and felt compassion for him, and ran and embraced him and kissed him, and said to his slaves, 'Quickly bring out the best robe and put it on him, and put a ring on his hand and sandals on his feet; and bring the fattened calf, kill it, and let us eat and celebrate; for this son of mine was dead and has come to life again; he was lost and has been found.' And they began to celebrate."

However, the older son did not like this and in anger said to his father,

> "Look! For so many years I have been serving you and I have never neglected a command of yours; and yet you have never given me a young goat, so that I might celebrate with my friends; but when this son of yours came, who has devoured your wealth with prostitutes, you killed the fattened calf for him."

The older son did not love being with the father, he served him and obeyed him, but only to receive his inheritance. Both sons had to humble themselves and genuinely want to love and be with their father. And we must do the same! We must humble ourselves, like the younger son did, before being accepted into the Father's Kingdom!

The questions we all need to ask ourselves are:
> ➢ Do I believe what the Bible says?
> ➢ Do I want to change the direction I am going in life?
> ➢ Do I want to go through the gate that leads to eternal life and become a follower of Jesus Christ?
> ➢ Or do I want to continue down the path I am on now?

*We can surrender our lives to Jesus Christ
and move closer to God,
or we can remain in our pride and move away from God.
The choice is up to each one of us,
and so are the consequences!*

If you would like to make this life changing decision it is important to believe all we have said as summarized below. To follow Jesus Christ:

➢ You need to truly and humbly admit to God that you are a sinner who needs salvation. When Isaiah felt the reality of his sin and need for salvation he said,

"Woe to me!" I cried. "I am ruined! For I am a man of unclean lips, and I live among a people of unclean lips, and my eyes have seen the King, the LORD Almighty."[a]

➢ You must desire to turn from your sins (repent), enter a relationship with God through faith in Jesus Christ, and live a new life as a follower of Jesus Christ.

➢ You must believe that God, in the person of Jesus Christ, died for you on the cross to pay for your sins and rose from the grave conquering death.

➢ Through prayer you need to invite Jesus Christ into your life and receive him as your Savior and Lord.

As you think about your decision and pray about it, you are invited to read the following prayers.

An Invitation to Christ by Dmitri of Rostov

Come, my Light, and illumine my darkness.
Come, my Life, and revive me from death.
Come, my Physician, and heal my wounds.
Come, Flame of divine love,
and burn up the thorns of my sins,
kindling my heart with the flame of your love.
Come, my King, sit upon the throne of my heart
and reign there.
For You alone are my King and my Lord.

A Song of Penitence
Prayer of Manasseh 1-2, 4, 6-7, 11-15

While a prisoner, Manasseh prayed for mercy, and upon being freed and restored to the throne turned from his idolatress ways. A reference to the prayer, but not the prayer itself, is made

---

[a] Isaiah 6:5

49

in 2 Chronicles[a], which says that the prayer is written in "the annals of the kings of Israel". The prayer is considered apocryphal by Jews, Catholics, and Protestants.

> O Lord and Ruler of the hosts of heaven,
> God of Abraham, Isaac, and Jacob,
> and of all their righteous offspring:
> You made the heavens and the earth,
> with all their vast array.
> All things quake with fear at your presence;
> they tremble because of your power.
> But your merciful promise is beyond all measure;
> it surpasses all that our minds can fathom.
> O Lord, you are full of compassion,
> long-suffering, and abounding in mercy.
> You hold back your hand;
> you do not punish as we deserve.
> In your great goodness, Lord,
> you have promised forgiveness to sinners,
> that they may repent of their sin and be saved.
> And now, O Lord, I bend the knee of my heart,
> and make my appeal, sure of your gracious goodness.
> I have sinned, O Lord, I have sinned,
> and I know my wickedness only too well.
> Therefore I make this prayer to you:
> Forgive me, Lord, forgive me.
> Do not let me perish in my sin,
> nor condemn me to the depths of the earth.
> For you, O Lord, are the God of those who repent,
> and in me you will show forth your goodness.
> Unworthy as I am, you will save me,
> in accordance with your great mercy,
> and I will praise you without ceasing all the days of my life.
> For all the powers of heaven sing your praises,
> and yours is the glory to ages of ages. Amen.

---

[a] 2 Chronicles 33:15–17

PRAYING TO RECEIVE JESUS CHRIST AS SAVIOR AND LORD

I keep the picture on the left on my desk to remind me that I need to often kneel before my Lord and daily give myself to him, for Jesus himself is the only gate and pathway into paradise! It was made by using a forge and hammered out by a man in one of my churches, who later became a pastor. It was a privilege and a blessing to see the Lord work in his life!

If you believe in your heart, even if you do not fully understand it, all that was said so far in this book, and you have a desire to have a personal relationship with Jesus; then say the following prayer, or in your own words repent and confess Jesus Christ as your Savior and Lord.

I come before you O God, I confess that I am a sinner and deserve eternal separation from you. I believe that you sent your Son Jesus to earth as a man to save me. I believe that Jesus lived a perfect life for me. I believe that he died on the cross to pay for my sins and rose from the grave three days later conquering death. I thank you Jesus for dying on the cross for me to pay for my sins! Please forgive me for all my sins! Right now, in the best way I know how, I open the door of my heart and life and receive you as my Savior and Lord! Fill me with your Holy Spirit. Take over the control of my life. Change me from the inside out. Make me the type of person you created me to be. Thank you for coming into my life by faith! Thank you for saving me! Amen.

The Assurance of Salvation

The love and power of God has been working in your life to bring you to this moment! Believing and praying the above prayer to receive Jesus Christ is all it takes to become a forgiven child of God.

When we believe in and receive Jesus Christ as Lord and Savior the Bible reveals that some life changing events take place. As the following verses declare.

➤ Your sins are forgiven! Your guilt is removed!

"If we say that we have no sin, we are deceiving ourselves

and the truth is not in us. If we confess our sins, He is faithful and righteous to forgive us our sins and to cleanse us from all unrighteousness."[a]

"How blessed is he whose transgression is forgiven, whose sin is covered! How blessed is the man to whom the Lord does not impute iniquity, and in whose spirit there is no deceit! When I kept silent about my sin, my body wasted away through my groaning all day long. For day and night Your hand was heavy upon me; my vitality was drained away as with the fever heat of summer. I acknowledged my sin to You, and my iniquity I did not hide; I said, 'I will confess my transgressions to the Lord'; and You forgave the guilt of my sin. Therefore, let everyone who is godly pray to You in a time when You may be found; surely in a flood of great waters they will not reach him. You are my hiding place; You preserve me from trouble; You surround me with songs of deliverance. I will instruct you and teach you in the way which you should go; I will counsel you with My eye upon you. Do not be as the horse or as the mule which have no understanding, whose trappings include bit and bridle to hold them in check, otherwise they will not come near to you. Many are the sorrows of the wicked, but he who trusts in the Lord, lovingkindness shall surround him. Be glad in the Lord and rejoice, you righteous ones; and shout for joy, all you who are upright in heart."[b]

"As far as the east is from the west, so far has He removed our transgressions from us."[c]

"In Him we have redemption through His blood, the forgiveness of our trespasses, according to the riches of His grace which He lavished on us."[d]

"For I will be merciful to their iniquities, and I will remember their sins no more."[e]

---

[a] 1 John 1:8–9 (NAS)
[b] Psalm 32:1–11 (See also Psalm 38)
[c] Psalm 103:11–13
[d] Ephesians 1:7–8
[e] Hebrews 8:12

> ➢ You are saved!

"Everyone who calls on the name of the Lord will be saved."[a]

> ➢ You have become a child of God!

"But as many as received Him, to them He gave the right to become children of God, even to those who believe in His name, who were born, not of blood nor of the will of the flesh nor of the will of man, but of God."[b]

> ➢ The Spirit of God lives in you!

"The Spirit himself testifies with our spirit that we are children of God,"[c]

"In Him, you also, after listening to the message of truth, the gospel of your salvation—having also believed, you were sealed in Him with the Holy Spirit of promise, who is given as a pledge of our inheritance, with a view to the redemption of God's own possession, to the praise of His glory."[d]

> ➢ You now have the hope of a wonderful life with God for the rest of your life!

"Blessed be the God and Father of our Lord Jesus Christ, who has blessed us with every spiritual blessing in the heavenly places in Christ, just as He chose us in Him before the foundation of the world, that we would be holy and blameless before Him. In love He predestined us to adoption as sons through Jesus Christ to Himself, according to the kind intention of His will, You have the promise of a place in paradise for all eternity."[e]

> ➢ You are part of the Church (God's people, the Body of Christ)!

"Now you are Christ's body, and individually members of it."[f]

---

[a] Romans 10:13
[b] John 1:12–13
[c] Romans 8:16
[d] Ephesians 1:13–14
[e] Ephesians 1:3–5
[f] 1 Corinthians 12:27

➢ And the process of transforming your life has begun!

"Therefore, brethren, since we have confidence to enter the holy place by the blood of Jesus, by a new and living way which He inaugurated for us through the veil, that is, His flesh, and since we have a great priest over the house of God, let us draw near with a sincere heart in full assurance of faith, having our hearts sprinkled clean from an evil conscience and our bodies washed with pure water. Let us hold fast the confession of our hope without wavering, for He who promised is faithful; and let us consider how to stimulate one another to love and good deeds, not forsaking our own assembling together, as is the habit of some, but encouraging one another; and all the more as you see the day drawing near."[a]

All this is accomplished through the supernatural work of the Holy Spirit who indwells every believer. This is called *regeneration*, or the "new birth." In God's eyes you are now *justified*, you are saved from the guilt and penalty of sin! As it declares in Romans "Therefore there is now no condemnation for those who are in Christ Jesus."[b] You might want to read and meditate on Psalm 103 that celebrates the wonderful things that God in love has done for us, and what he calls us to!

John Newton, the captain of a slave ship in the British slave trade business, wrote this song when he was saved after the Holy Spirit worked in his life to make him aware of the need for salvation.

"Amazing Grace"

Amazing grace! How sweet the sound
that saved a wretch like me!
I once was lost, but now am found;
was blind, but now I see.

'Twas grace that taught my heart to fear,
and grace my fears relieved;
how precious did that grace appear
the hour I first believed.

---

[a] Hebrews 10:19–25
[b] Romans 8:1, read all of Romans 8 to delve into this remarkable truth!

Through many dangers, toils, and snares,
I have already come;
'tis grace hath brought me safe thus far,
and grace will lead me home.

The Lord has promised good to me,
his word my hope secures;
he will my shield and portion be,
as long as life endures.

Yea, when this flesh and heart shall fail,
and mortal life shall cease,
I shall possess, within the veil,
a life of joy and peace.

When we've been there ten thousand years,
bright shining as the sun,
we've no less days to sing God's praise
than when we'd first begun.

Charles Wesley wrote the following song after he received the assurance of the forgiveness of his sins and was overcome with joy!

"And Can It Be that I Should Gain"

And can it be that I should gain
an interest in the Savior's blood!
Died he for me? who caused His pain!
For me? who him to death pursued?
Amazing love! How can it be
that thou, my God, shouldst die for me?
Amazing love! How can it be
that thou, my God, shouldst die for me?

'Tis mystery all: th' Immortal dies!
Who can explore His strange design?
In vain the firstborn seraph tries
to sound the depths of love divine.
'Tis mercy all! Let earth adore;
let angel minds inquire no more.
'Tis mercy all! Let earth adore;
let angel minds inquire no more.

He left His Father's throne above
(so free, so infinite His grace!),
emptied himself of all but love,
and bled for Adam's helpless race.
'Tis mercy all, immense and free,
for O my God, it found out me!
'Tis mercy all, immense and free,
for O my God, it found out me!

Long my imprisoned spirit lay,
fast bound in sin and nature's night;
thine eye diffused a quickening ray;
I woke, the dungeon flamed with light;
my chains fell off, my heart was free,
I rose, went forth, and followed thee.
My chains fell off, my heart was free,
I rose, went forth, and followed thee.

No condemnation now I dread;
Jesus, and all in him, is mine;
alive in him, my living Head,
and clothed in righteousness divine,
bold I approach th' eternal throne,
and claim the crown, through Christ my own.
Bold I approach th' eternal throne,
and claim the crown, through Christ my own.

Baptized into God's Kingdom

After receiving Jesus Christ as Lord and Savior, baptism "in the name of the Father and of the Son and of the Holy Spirit"[a] should follow. Baptism, immersed by water in the name of the Father, Son, and Holy Spirit, into a new life as a follower of Jesus Christ, is a sacrament, a means of divine grace, or a sign or symbol of a spiritual reality, that is a public declaration as being a follower of Jesus Christ and part of his Church.

Baptism should be thought of as not just acceptance of Christ and becoming a Christian. It is the beginning of a journey. In fact,

---

[a] Matthew 28:19, Acts 22:16

think of the rest of life as "living into our baptism." To "live into our baptism" means to live in such a way that a transformation from being self-focused and having personal agendas, to being people who forget self and live a rich Christ centered life with other Christians. This new life God calls us to live is a life empowered by the Holy Spirit where patterns of living that hurt or weaken relationships are rejected and, instead, living together as forgiven, healed, and transformed people is the desired behavior. Together new Christian should support, encourage, and build up one another while seeking and serving God.[a]

During your confession of faith in Jesus Christ, as declared in baptism, the following happened: God judged your fallen rebellious nature, and your sinful practices that flow from it, by absorbing them into himself and judging himself instead of you. Then, instead of judging you he reached out in mercy with the offer of grace, forgiveness, the Holy Spirit, and a new life! Once you have received Christ as your Savior and have been baptized, often an invitation to join a local church is extended by taking the membership class and repeating the membership vows before God and your church family.

What does it mean to 'live into our baptism' as Charles Wesley wrote in, "Come, Let Us Use the Grace Divine?"

> Come, let us use the grace divine,
> and all with one accord,
> in a perpetual covenant
> join ourselves to Christ the Lord;
> Give up ourselves, thru Jesus' power,
> his name to glorify;
> and promise, in this sacred hour,
> for God to live and die.
>
> The covenant we this moment make
> be ever kept in mind; we will no more our God forsake,
> or cast these words behind.
> We never will throw off the fear
> of God who hears our vow;
> and if thou art well pleased to hear,

---

[a] see Romans 6:1-14

come down and meet us now.

Thee, Father, Son, and Holy Ghost,
let all our hearts receive,
present with thy celestial host
the peaceful answer give;
to each covenant the blood apply
which takes our sins away,
and register our names on high
and keep us to that day!

Chapter 6

The Journey Continues

The love of God that redeems my soul is "so amazing, so divine, (it) demands my soul, my life, my all." This phrase is in the following song by Isaac Watts,

"When I Survey the Wondrous Cross"

When I survey the wondrous cross
On which the Prince of Glory died,
My richest gain I count but loss,
And pour contempt on all my pride.

Forbid it, Lord, that I should boast,
Save in the death of Christ my God:
All the vain things that charm me most,
I sacrifice them to his blood.

See from his head, his hands, his feet,
Sorrow and love flow mingled down;
Did e'er such love and sorrow meet,
Or thorns compose so rich a crown?

His dying crimson, like a robe,
Spreads o'er His body on the tree;
Then I am dead to all the globe,
And all the globe is dead to me.

Were the whole realm of nature mine,
That were a present far too small;
Love so amazing, so divine,
Demands my soul, my life, my all.

So, what does it mean to give God "my soul, my life, my all"? A great clue is found in Ephesians which summarizes what God has done for humanity, and how believers are to respond to this wonderful gift of love and mercy.

"And you were dead in the trespasses and sins in which you once walked, following the course of this world, following the prince of the power of the air, the spirit that is now at work in the sons of disobedience— among whom we all once lived in the passions of our flesh, carrying out the desires of the body and the mind, and were by nature children of wrath, like the rest of mankind. But God, being rich in mercy, because of the great love with which He loved us, even when we were dead in our trespasses, made us alive together with Christ—by grace you have been saved— and raised us up with him and seated us with him in he heavenly places in Christ Jesus, so that in the coming ages he might show the immeasurable riches of his grace in kindness toward us in Christ Jesus. For by grace you have been saved through faith. And this is not your own doing; it is the gift of God, not a result of works, so that no one may boast. For we are his workmanship, created in Christ Jesus for good works, which God prepared beforehand, that we should walk in them."[a]

As a response to the gift of salvation God has given us, he calls us to begin the lifelong journey of following Jesus Christ. This journey is described by Jesus as a walk, a road, or path, which is narrow, meaning to be careful not to veer from it. It is a journey of making baptism a reality in daily life. This journey with Jesus is what salvation is all about and is called *sanctification,* where we are saved from the power of sin. *The goal of sanctification is to go on the lifelong journey of progressively becoming more like Jesus Christ inwardly in our character and outwardly in our actions and growing in our love for God and people.* As the song above says, Jesus's love is, "so amazing, so divine, (it) demands my soul, my life, my all!"

Sanctification can be described as walking in the footsteps of Christ as seen in these Scriptures, a song, and the quotes from a few Christian leaders throughout history.

When he had sinned King David cried out to God saying, "Be gracious to me, O God, according to Your lovingkindness; according to the greatness of Your

---

[a] Ephesians 2:1-10 (EVS)

compassion blot out my transgressions. Wash me thoroughly from my iniquity an cleanse me from my sin. For I know my transgressions, and my sin is ever before me. Against You, You only, I have sinned and done what is evil in Your sight, so that You are justified when You speak and blameless when You judge. ... Hide Your face from my sins and blot out all my iniquities. Create in me a clean heart, O God, and renew a steadfast spirit within me. Do not cast me away from Your presence and do not take Your Holy Spirit from me. Restore to me the joy of Your salvation and sustain me with a willing spirit. Then I will teach transgressors Your ways, and sinners will be converted to You."[a]

"Righteousness will go before him and make him footsteps a way."[b]

"My son, do not forget my teaching,
But let your heart keep my commandments;
For length of days and years of life
And peace they will add to you.
 Do not let kindness and truth leave you;
Bind them around your neck,
Write them on the tablet of your heart."[c]

"For thus says the high and exalted One who lives forever, whose name is Holy, 'I dwell on a high and holy place, and also with the contrite and lowly of spirit in order to revive the spirit of the lowly and to revive the heart of the contrite.'"[d]

"Do nothing from selfishness or empty conceit, but with humility of mind regard one another as more important than yourselves; do not merely look out for your own personal interests, but also for the interests of others. Have this attitude in yourselves which was also in Christ Jesus, who, although he existed in the form of God, did not regard equality with God a thing to be grasped, but emptied Himself, taking the form of a bond-servant, and being made

---

[a] Psalm 51:1-4, 9-13
[b] Psalm 85:13
[c] Proverbs 3:1–3
[d] Isaiah 57:15

in the likeness of men. Being found in appearance as a man, he humbled himself by becoming obedient to the point of death, even death on a cross."[a]

"Therefore, my dear friends, as you have always obeyed, not only in my presence, but now much more in my absence, continue to work out your salvation with fear and trembling, for it is God who works in you to will and to act according to his good purpose."[b]

"Now those who belong to Christ Jesus have crucified the flesh with its passions and desires. If we live by the Spirit, let us also walk by the Spirit."[c]

"Pursue peace with all men, and the sanctification without which no one will see the Lord."[d]

"By this we know that we are in Him: whoever says he abides in Him ought to walk in the same way in which He walked."[e]

"For a Heart to Praise My God" by Charles Wesley

O for a heart to praise my God,
a heart from sin set free,
a heart that always feels thy blood
so freely shed for me.
A heart resigned, submissive, meek,
my great Redeemer's throne,
where only Christ is heard to speak,
where Jesus reigns alone.

A humble, lowly, contrite heart,
believing, true, and clean,
which neither life nor death can part
from Christ who dwells within.

---

[a] Philippians 2:3-8
[b] Philippians. 2:12-13 (NIV)
[c] Galatians 5:24-25 (NAS), Also read Galatians 5,
Ephesians 4-6, and 2 Corinthians 5:1-6:10
[d] Hebrews 12:14
[e] 1 John 2:5-6

A heart in every thought renewed
and full of love divine,
perfect and right and pure and good,
a copy, Lord, of thine.

Thy nature, gracious Lord, impart;
come quickly from above;
write thy new name upon my heart,
thy new, best name of Love.

In about 400 A.D. Augustine said,

But I am struggling to return from this 'far country' (Luke 15:31) by the road He has made in the humanity of the divinity of His only Son.[7]

Then, about a thousand years later Thomas à Kempis, wrote,

What a debt of gratitude I owe you, for your mercy in showing me, along with all your faithful followers, the straight and true road that leads to your eternal kingdom! That road we must follow is your own life; by holy patience we make our way towards you; you who are to crown our journey. Had you not gone before and shown us the way, which of us would care to follow it? Many, I fear, would stay behind, remain at a distance, if they had not your wondrous example to gaze at. Why, even now, for all the times we have heard of your teaching and all your miracles, the flame within us burns low; what would happen if we lacked the great glow of light to guide us in following you?[8]

For our final example John Wesley in the 1700's wrote,

I have thought, I am a creature of a day, passing through life as an arrow through the air. I am a spirit come from God, and returning to God; just hovering over this great gulf till in a few moments hence, I am no more seen, I drop into an unchangeable eternity! I want to know one thing, the way to heaven; how to land safe on that happy shore. God himself has condescended to teach the way, for this very end he came from heaven. He has written it down in a book. O give me that book! At any price give me the book of God! I have it; here is knowledge enough for me. Let me be a man of one book. Here then I am, far from the busy ways of men. I sit down alone. Only God is here. In His presence I open it, I read His book, for this end, to find the way to heaven.[9]

A question we must ask ourselves is, "Why don't most of us have this passion as seen in these three men and millions of other men and women throughout Christian history?" A. W. Tozer gave a good answer in his explanation of sanctification when he said,

> Simply, he [sinful man] must repent and believe. … The cross that ended the earthly life of Jesus now puts an end to the sinner; and the power that raised Christ from the dead now raises him to a new life along with Christ.[10]

The reward of this journey is eternal life as seen in Romans,

> "But now having been freed from sin and enslaved to God, you derive your benefit, resulting in sanctification, and the outcome, eternal life."[a]

Being a follower of Christ must be lived out among God's people, who are the church.[b] When thinking of the church it is important to have a proper view of who she is and why she exists. The church must be viewed as the gathered people of God who have come to faith in Jesus Christ. In our life together there is a need to help each other grow in faith, focus on worship, fellowship, take the sacraments, pray, study, witness, and serve in the church and community. As we make this life together a priority in our lives, God will heal and transform our hearts and minds into the image of Christ as seen in these verses when Jesus tells us why he came,

> "The Spirit of the Lord is upon Me, because He anointed Me to preach the gospel to the poor. He has sent Me to proclaim release to the captives and recovery of sight to the blind, to set free those who are oppressed. To proclaim the accepted and acceptable year of the Lord."[c]

In the Greek language this verse means something like, "The Spirit of the Lord is upon Me, because He anointed Me *(the*

---

[a] Romans 6:22
[b] By saying 'church' I mean the true believers in and followers of Jesus Christ throughout history.
[c] Luke 4:18-19

Anointed One, the Messiah) to preach the gospel *(the glad tidings of the coming kingdom of God, of the salvation to be obtained in it through Christ, and all the benefits that relates to this salvation)* to the poor *(the lowly, afflicted, and destitute of the Christian virtues and eternal riches).* He has sent Me to proclaim release to the captives, and recovery of sight to the blind *(to blunt the mental discernment, darken the mind),* to set free those who are oppressed *(who are downtrodden, bruised, crushed, and broken down by calamity).* To proclaim the accepted and acceptable year of the Lord *(the day when salvation and the free favors of God profusely abound.)*"

Living together as God's people, our greatest hope and passion comes when on the final day of history when the church's Bridegroom, who is Jesus Christ, returns and says, "Well done good and faithful servant." He will say this to all who have made him their first love and focused on growing his kingdom within their self and served him in the world for his glory. The Bible speaks of this future hope we have in verses such as,

"Do not let your heart be troubled; believe in God, believe also in Me. In My Father's house are many dwelling places; if it were not so, I would have told you; for I go to prepare a place for you. If I go and prepare a place for you, I will come again and receive you to Myself, that where I am, there you may be also."[a]

"And without faith it is impossible to please Him, for he who comes to God must believe that He is and that He is a rewarder of those who seek Him. ... (Abraham) was looking for the city which has foundations, whose architect and builder is God. ... All these died in faith, without receiving the promises, but having seen them and having welcomed them from a distance, and having confessed that they were strangers and exiles on the earth. For those who say such things make it clear that they are seeking a country of their own. And indeed if they had been thinking of that country from which they went out, they would have had opportunity

---

[a] John 14:1-3

to return. But as it is, they desire a better country, that is, a heavenly one. Therefore God is not ashamed to be called their God; for He has prepared a city for them."[a]

"Therefore if you have been raised up with Christ, keep seeking the things above, where Christ is, seated at the right hand of God. Set your mind on the things above, not on the things that are on earth. For you have died and your life is hidden with Christ in God. When Christ, who is our life, is revealed, then you also will be revealed with him in glory."[b]

"For our citizenship is in heaven, from which also we eagerly wait for a Savior, the Lord Jesus Christ;"[c]

John Wesley had an amazing experience on his journey of sanctification in 1738 that caused him to say, "I felt my heart strangely warmed." This experience began a few years earlier when he traveled to Savanna, Georgia to minister to the Native Americans. He left England for America on October 14, 1735 on a four-month journey across the Atlantic Ocean, during which they encountered three fierce storms in January of 1736.

During the second storm Wesley stepped out of his cabin and was immediately overwhelmed by at huge wave and later asked himself, "How it is that thou hast no faith? Why am I being still unwilling to die?" It seemed that he did not have a faith that fully trusted his entire life to Christ no matter what happened, even when faced with death itself.

Two days later, on January 25th, a third storm, worse than the first two, hit them. After the storm Wesley wrote about the difference between the reactions of the English and Moravian Germans in his journal by writing,

> "A terrible screaming began among the English. The Germans calmly sang on. I asked one of them afterward, 'Were you not afraid?' He answered, 'I thank God, no.' I asked, 'But were not your women and children afraid?' He replied, mildly, 'No; our women and children are not afraid to die."

---

[a] Hebrews 11:6, 10, 13-16
[b] Colossians 3:1-4
[c] Philippians 3:20

Wesley arrived in Savannah, Georgia on February 6, 1736 and served in America for two years. His ministry did not go well in America and on February 29, 1738 Wesley arrived back in England. After he returned Wesley wrote the following evaluation of his ministry in America in his journal,

> "I went to America, to convert the Indians; but oh! who shall convert me? who, what is he that will deliver me from this evil heart of mischief? I have a fair summer religion. I can talk well; nay, and believe myself, while no danger is near; but let death look me in the face, and my spirit is troubled. Nor can I say, 'To die is gain!'

Wesley was still struggling with the experience on the ship to America, and how he felt about his ministry there. He felt that his faith was not strong enough to say, 'To die is gain!' Then, in May of 1738 he wrote the following in his Journal describing an amazing experience on his journey of sanctification that caused him to say, "I felt my heart strangely warmed."

> "When I met Peter Bohler again, he consented to put the dispute upon the issue which I desired, namely, scripture and experience. I first consulted the scripture. But when I set aside the glosses of men, and simply considered the words of God, comparing them together, endeavoring to illustrate the obscure by the plainer passages; I found they all made against me, and was forced to retreat to my last hold, "that experience would never agree with the *literal interpretation* of those scriptures. Nor could I therefore allow it to be true, till I found some living witnesses of it." He replied, he could show me such at any time; if I desired it, the next day. And accordingly, the next day he came again with three others, all of whom testified, of their own personal experience, that a true living faith in Christ is inseparable from a sense of pardon for all past, and freedom from all present, sins. They added with one mouth, that this faith was the gift, the free gift of God; and that he would surely bestow it upon every soul who earnestly and perseveringly sought it. I was now thoroughly convinced; and, by the grace of God, I resolved to seek it unto the end,
>
> 1. By absolutely renouncing all dependence, in whole or in part, upon *my own* works or righteousness; on which I had really grounded my hope of salvation though I knew it not,

from my youth up.

2. By adding to the constant use of all the other means of grace, continual prayer for this very thing, justifying, saving faith, a full reliance on the blood of Christ shed for *me;* a trust in Him, as *my* Christ, as *my* sole justification, sanctification, and redemption.

I continued thus to seek it, (though with strange indifference, dullness, and coldness, and unusually frequent relapses into sin,) till Wednesday, May 24. I think it was about five this morning, that I opened my Testament on those words, "There are given unto us exceeding great and precious promises, even that ye should be partakers of the divine nature." (2 Peter 1:4.) Just as I went out, I opened it again on those words, "Thou art not far from the kingdom of God." In the afternoon I was asked to go to St. Paul's. The anthem was, "Out of the deep have I called unto thee, O Lord: Lord, hear my voice. O let thine ears consider well the voice of my complaint. If thou, Lord, wilt be extreme to mark what is done amiss, O Lord, who may abide it? For there is mercy with thee; therefore shalt thou be feared. O Israel, trust in the Lord: For with the Lord there is mercy, and with him is plenteous redemption. And He shall redeem Israel from all his sins."

In the evening I went very unwillingly to a society in Aldersgate Street, where one was reading Luther's preface to the Epistle to the Romans. About a quarter before nine, while he was describing the change which God works in the heart through faith in Christ, I felt my heart strangely warmed. I felt I did trust in Christ, Christ alone for salvation: And an assurance was given me, that he had taken away *my* sins, even *mine,* and saved *me* from the law of sin and death.

I began to pray with all my might for those who had in a more especial manner despitefully used me and persecuted me. I then testified openly to all there, what I now first felt in my heart. But it was not long before the enemy suggested, 'This cannot be faith; for where is thy joy?' Then was I taught, that peace and victory over sin are essential to faith in the Captain of our salvation: But that, as to the transports of joy that usually attend the beginning of it, especially in those who have mourned deeply, God sometimes giveth, sometimes with holdeth them, according to the counsels of His own will.

After my return home, I was much buffeted with temptations; but cried out, and they fled away. They returned again and again. I as often lifted up my eyes, and He "sent me help from His holy place." And herein I found the difference between this and my former state chiefly consisted. I was striving, yea, fighting with all my might under the law, as well as under grace. But then I was sometimes, if not often, conquered; now, I was always conqueror.

Thur. 25. — The moment I awaked, "Jesus, Master," was in my heart and in my mouth; and I found all my strength lay in keeping my eye fixed upon him, and my soul waiting on him continually. Being again at St. Paul's in the afternoon, I could taste the good word of God in the anthem, which began, "My song shall be always of the loving kindness of the Lord: With my mouth will I ever be showing forth thy truth from one generation to another." Yet the enemy injected a fear, "If thou dost believe, why is there not a more sensible change?" I answered, (yet not I,) "That I know not. But this I know, I have 'now peace with God.' And I sin not today, and Jesus my Master has forbid me to take thought for the morrow."

"But is not any sort of fear," continued the tempter, "a proof that thou dost not believe?" I desired my Master to answer for me; and opened His Book upon those words of St. Paul, "Without were fightings, within were fears." Then, inferred I, well may fears be within me; but I must go on, and tread them under my feet." [11]

This experience from God was very profound in John Wesley's life! God used it to lead John and his brother Charles into a powerful ministry; a ministry that God used to touch millions of people around the world to this day! The following prayer by John Wesley speaks passionately of the journey of sanctification, which means growing in holiness of heart, soul, and mind to serve the Lord Jesus Christ.

"A Covenant Prayer in the Wesleyan Tradition" by John Wesley

I am no longer my own, but thine.
Put me to what thou wilt, rank me with whom thou wilt.
Put me to doing, put me to suffering.
Let me be employed for thee or laid aside for thee,
exalted for thee or brought low for thee.
Let me be full, let me be empty.
Let me have all things, let me have nothing.
I freely and heartily yield all things to thy pleasure and disposal.
And now, O glorious and blessed God,
Father, Son and Holy Spirit,
thou art mine, and I am thine. So be it.
And the covenant which I have made on earth,
let it be ratified in heaven. Amen.

When we think of sanctification we should ask, "But how to I become sanctified?" Paul gives us a clue when he said,

"I press on toward the goal for the prize of the upward call of God in Christ Jesus."[a]

That is what we will now explore on our journey of being a follower of Jesus. And as you and me "press on toward the goal" let us always remember that …

Jesus is *the* Light and *the* Truth who leads us to the path of life created by God and invites us to walk on it.

He will also be our guide on that narrow path of life that leads to paradise.

---

[a] Philippians 3:12-14

Chapter 7

Your Journey as a
Follower of Jesus

As you begin your life as a follower of Jesus Christ, you are following in the footsteps of countless men and women who over the centuries have fought for the Christian faith against many enemies. Part of the fight for the faith in the early church was to clearly proclaim what was believed as they defended the faith against those who sought to distort or destroy it. Two especially important statements of faith or creeds that were developed are *The Apostle's Creed* and *The Nicene Creed*.

The Apostle's Creed

"I believe in God, the Father Almighty,
    creator of heaven and earth.
I believe in Jesus Christ, His only Son, our Lord,
    who was conceived by the Holy Spirit,
    born of the Virgin Mary,
    suffered under Pontius Pilate,
    was crucified, died, and was buried;
    he descended to the dead.
    On the third day he rose again;
    he ascended into heaven,
    is seated at the right hand of the Father,
    and will come again to judge the living and the dead.
I believe in the Holy Spirit,
    the holy catholic church,
    the communion of saints,
    the forgiveness of sins,
    the resurrection of the body, and the life everlasting. Amen."

The Nicene Creed

"We believe in one God,
    the Father, the Almighty,
    maker of heaven and earth
    of all that is, seen and unseen.
We believe in one Lord, Jesus Christ,
    the only Son of God,
    eternally begotten of the Father,
    God from God, Light from Light,
    true God from true God,
    begotten, not made,
    of one Being with the Father;
    through him all things were made.
    For us and for our salvation.
    he came down from heaven,
    was incarnate of the Holy Spirit and the Virgin Mary
    and became truly human.
    For our sake he was crucified under Pontius Pilate;
    he suffered death and was buried.
    On the third day he rose again
    in accordance with the scriptures;
    he ascended into heaven
    and is seated at the right hand of the Father.
    He will come again in glory to judge the living and the dead,
    and His kingdom will have no end.
We believe in the Holy Spirit, the Lord, the giver of life,
    who proceeds from the Father and the Son,
    who with the Father and the Son is worshiped and glorified,
    who has spoken through the prophets.
We believe in one holy catholic and apostolic church.
    We acknowledge one baptism for the forgiveness of sins.
    We look for the resurrection of the dead,
    and the life of the world to come. Amen."

A good question to ask as you begin a life following Christ is, "Just how do I live my life as a follower of Jesus Christ? How do I walk by the Spirit as I work out my salvation, like the people who lived it out successfully throughout Christian history?"

To answer this question, it is important to be reminded that salvation is being saved from a life centered on self and being transformed into a person whose life is centered on God.

Just before his arrest Jesus prayed about the very reason he had come into the world when he said, "that they may all be one; even as You, Father, are in Me and I in You, that they also may be in Us, so that the world may believe that You sent Me."[a]

Jesus came so that mankind could have a relationship with God *and* relationships with each other that resemble in some way the relationship between the members of the Trinity.

Therefore, Christianity is a lifelong journey of transformation as you grow in your love for, knowledge of, relationship with, trust in, and obedience to Jesus Christ.

A growing relationship to Jesus will automatically include developing deep, loving relationships with other Christians, and to grow in knowledge of the ways of God and living them out in daily life in a fallen world. Bill and Annabel Gillman, in one of their books, speaks of living life according to the ways of the world is like driving on a superhighway; they are what we are used to and seems so natural. Now, as Christians we are leaving the superhighway and going on a new path that is narrow and against the ways of the world. The ways of life on this path are the ways of the Kingdom of God. They may be difficult, but they are good, the way God created us to live. As Jesus said,

"Enter through the narrow gate; for the gate is wide and the way is broad that leads to destruction, and there are many who enter through it. For the gate is small and the way is narrow that leads to life, and there are few who find it."[b]

A good summary of what the life of a follower of Christ should look like is seen in the following Scriptures.

"They were continually devoting themselves to the apostles' teaching and to fellowship, to the breaking of bread and to prayer. Everyone kept feeling a sense of awe; and many wonders and signs were taking place through the apostles. And all those who had believed were together and had all

---

[a] John 17:21
[b] Matthew 7:13–14

things in common; and they began selling their property and possessions and were sharing them with all, as anyone might have need. Day by day continuing with one mind in the temple, and breaking bread from house to house, they were taking their meals together with gladness and sincerity of heart," Acts 2:42-46

"Jesus replied: 'Love the Lord your God with all your heart and with all your soul and with all your mind.' This is the first and greatest commandment. And the second is like it: 'Love your neighbor as yourself.' All the Law and the Prophets hang on these two commandments."[a]

"And by this we know that we have come to know him, if we keep His commandments. Whoever says "I know him" but does not keep His commandments is a liar, and the truth is not in him, but whoever keeps His word, in him truly the love of God is perfected. By this we may know that we are in him:"[b]

"And He summoned the crowd with His disciples, and said to them, "If anyone wishes to come after Me, he must deny himself, and take up his cross and follow Me. For whoever wishes to save his life will lose it, but whoever loses his life for My sake and the gospel's will save it. For what does it profit a man to gain the whole world, and forfeit his soul? For what will a man give in exchange for his soul? For whoever is ashamed of Me and My words in this adulterous and sinful generation, the Son of Man will also be ashamed of him when He comes in the glory of His Father with the holy angels.'"[c]

In my study of the book of Mark I wrote the following on what I think these verses above say to all of us.

"Now a choice must be made: which one will I follow? Between now and Christ's return what will be the course of my life? Christ is looking at each one of us and asking, 'Do you want to come after Me? If so, you must deny yourself,

---

[a] Matthew 22:37-40 (NIV)
[b] 1 John 2:3–5
[c] Mark 8:34–38 (NAS)

take up your cross and follow Me.'

My life is not about me, it is about Christ and the Gospel, it is about proclaiming the life, death, and resurrection of Christ and the new life he brings as I die to self and live for Christ. Only then is my life truly saved: saved from self and living in the freedom of a servant and child of the King of kings. This is what it means to 'take up his cross and follow Christ.'

The world is fleeting and passing away. So, what if I have wealth, popularity, knowledge of those fleeting things? They will be gone and been of no benefit to my soul! I have nothing to offer God that will save my soul. What should I do? Nothing but throw myself at the feet of Christ and rise-up to live in loving obedience to him, the Savior of my soul!

Am I ashamed of Jesus and his words? Do I live and proclaim them boldly? We certainly live in a time filled with adulterous and sinful people, a people who reject Christ for lesser things. Even most in the church love self and their own wisdom more than Christ and his ways. For Christians to do this reveals they are living in idolatry for they have left, or never known, Christ as their first love. We must ask ourselves: Is Christ ashamed of how I live and proclaim my faith?"

These verses above describe a life that was different from the life the early believers had been living. It was a way of life that revolved around understanding and living out the teachings of Jesus and the early Christian leaders as found in the New Testament. Their lives revolved around a deep personal relationship with God *and* deep relationships with each other. In other words, it was, and still should be, a simple life which focuses on loving and following Jesus with a reality and power that demonstrates itself in love and care for each other.

A well-balanced Christian walk is a life drawing closer and closer to Jesus, and as a result growing in our love for him and his ways of life. And, as a result we grow less and less in love with the ways of the flesh and the world, and seek to glorify God in all we think, say, and do. These verses from Isaiah and Psalm 25 say it well,

Isaiah 55:6–12
"Seek the Lord while He may be found;
Call upon Him while He is near.
Let the wicked forsake His way
And the unrighteous man His thoughts;
And let him return to the Lord,
And He will have compassion on him,
And to our God,
For He will abundantly pardon.
'For My thoughts are not your thoughts,
Nor are your ways My ways,' declares the Lord.
'For as the heavens are higher than the earth,
So are My ways higher than your ways
And My thoughts than your thoughts.
For as the rain and the snow come down from heaven,
And do not return there without watering the earth
And making it bear and sprout,
And furnishing seed to the sower and bread to the eater;
So will My word be which goes forth from My mouth;
It will not return to Me empty,
Without accomplishing what I desire,
And without succeeding in the matter for which I sent it.
For you will go out with joy and be led forth with peace;
The mountains and the hills will break forth into
shouts of joy before you,
And all the trees of the field will clap their hands.'"

Psalm 25:1-2a, 3-22
"To you, O Lord, I lift up my soul.
O my God, in you I trust; …
Make me to know your ways, O Lord;
teach me your paths.
Lead me in your truth and teach me,
for you are the God of my salvation;
for you I wait all the day long.
Remember your mercy, O Lord, and your steadfast love,
for they have been from of old.
Remember not the sins of my youth or my transgressions;
according to your steadfast love remember me,
for the sake of your goodness, O Lord!

76

Good and upright is the Lord;
therefore he instructs sinners in the way.
He leads the humble in what is right,
and teaches the humble his way.
All the paths of the Lord are steadfast love and faithfulness,
for those who keep his covenant and his testimonies.
For your name's sake, O Lord,
pardon my guilt, for it is great.
Who is the man who fears the Lord?
Him will he instruct in the way that he should choose.
His soul shall abide in well-being,
The friendship of the Lord is for those who fear him,
and he makes known to them his covenant.
My eyes are ever toward the Lord,
for he will pluck my feet out of the net.
Turn to me and be gracious to me,
for I am lonely and afflicted.
The troubles of my heart are enlarged;
bring me out of my distresses.
Consider my affliction and my trouble,
and forgive all my sins.
Consider how many are my foes,
and with what violent hatred they hate me.
Oh, guard my soul, and deliver me!
Let me not be put to shame, for I take refuge in you.
May integrity and uprightness preserve me,
for I wait for you."

The developing of a well-balanced Christian life reflects, but is certainly not limited to, the following habits, priorities, and virtues, that God uses to develop holiness within us. The habits, or disciplines, help us maintain a deep and growing relationship with God, and are covered in, "A Journey of Developing a Deep Relationship with God." Then, maintaining these basic habits we grow in our understanding and practice of living a godly life as covered in the next four chapters. As a result of this life, we develop Christ like virtues, some of them are covered in the next three chapters. These habits, priorities and virtues enable us to live as citizens of the Kingdom of God as described in the next chapter, "Living a Blessed Life as Seen in Ephesians," as we serve Christ in our marriages, our family, the church, and the world. In the next chapter, "Taking Holy Communion: The Journey in Sacrament," is about the celebration of Holy Communion which Jesus Christ instituted just before his crucifixion. Finally, the last chapter, "The Beginning of the Real Journey," looks at what the journey is ultimately all about.

This is what makes us 'fit for heaven' as we 'press on to maturity,' as declared to us in Hebrews 6:1-12, and in the following Psalm, and prayer. I encourage you to read and meditate on them before you go on to the next chapter.

Psalm 121
I lift up my eyes to the hills.
From where does my help come?
My help comes from the Lord,
who made heaven and earth.
He will not let your foot be moved;
he who keeps you will not slumber.
Behold, he who keeps Israel
will neither slumber nor sleep.
The Lord is your keeper;
the Lord is your shade on your right hand.
The sun shall not strike you by day,
nor the moon by night.
The Lord will keep you from all evil;
he will keep your life.
The Lord will keep
your going out and your coming in
from this time forth and forevermore.

For True Life by St. Teresa of Ávila

Govern all by your wisdom, O Lord,
so that I may always be serving you
as you desire and not as I choose.
Do not punish me, I ask,
by granting what I wish or ask,
if it offends your love that would always live in me.
Let me die to myself that I may serve you.
Let me live to you who in yourself are the true life. Amen

Chapter 8

A Journey of Developing a Deep Relationship with God

As I said above, as a Christian it is important to know that once we have made the decision to receive Christ as Savior, we must now follow him as our Lord. It is comforting to know that we have many people who have gone on the journey of following Christ before us, and who are cheering us on as we go on the same journey they went on, as the following verses from Hebrew declare to us.

"Therefore, since we have so great a cloud of witnesses surrounding us, let us also lay aside every encumbrance and the sin which so easily entangles us, and let us run with endurance the race that is set before us, fixing our eyes on Jesus, the author and perfecter of faith, who for the joy set before Him endured the cross, despising the shame, and has sat down at the right hand of the throne of God. For consider Him who has endured such hostility by sinners against Himself, so that you will not grow weary and lose heart."[a]

As followers of Christ our deepest desire must be to grow in our love for God and our obedience to Him. This passionate pursuit and loving obedience are seen in Scriptures such as,

"With all my heart I have sought You; do not let me wander from Your commandments. Your word I have treasured in my heart, that I may not sin against You."[b]

"By this we know that we have come to know Him, if we keep His commandments. The one who says, 'I have come to know Him,' and does not keep His commandments, is a liar, and the truth is not in him; but whoever keeps His word, in

---

[a] Hebrews 12:1-3 (NAS)
[b] Psalm 119:10-11

79

him the love of God has truly been perfected. By this we know that we are in Him: the one who says he abides in him ought himself to walk in the same manner as he walked."[a]

As we pursue a deeper relationship with Christ, we will develop a growing desire to have God transform our lives and make us more Christlike in our character, attitude, and actions. A good picture of this is found in the book of Jeremiah when God says,

> "Behold, like the clay in the potter's hand, so are you in My hand, O house of Israel."[b]

What God is saying in this verse is that he wants us to allow him to shape our lives like a potter shapes a piece of clay. Some of the habits, or spiritual disciplines, that God uses to help us experience his grace, transform our lives, and help us become intimate with him are:

- Daily talking to God in prayer - This section teaches about the need for a balanced prayer life, a prayer life following the pattern of the Lord's Prayer, ideas I use in my own prayer life, and a suggestion for a prayer life based on the pattern used in the Morning and Evening Prayers for many centuries
- Reading, meditating on, and studying the Bible daily
- Worshiping at least weekly with other Christians
- Developing deep relationships with other Christians
- Living the Sermon on the Mount as an expression of a genuine Christian life

Daily Talking to God in Prayer

THE NEED FOR A BALANCED PRAYER LIFE

Prayer is a wonderful gift God has given us that will transform our lives, and the world. Prayer allows us to talk with God, receive his strength and guidance, and connect with his thoughts, passions, and desires. The Bible says this, and much more, about prayer.

"Do not be anxious about anything, but in everything, by

---

[a] 1 John 2:3-6, see also Jeremiah 29:11-13
[b] Jeremiah 18:6

prayer and petition, with thanksgiving, present your requests to God. And the peace of God, which transcends all understanding, will guard your hearts and your minds in Christ Jesus."[a]

"Ask and it will be given to you; seek and you will find; knock and the door will be opened to you. For everyone who asks receives; he who seeks finds; and to him who knocks, the door will be opened."[b]

"And when he had taken it, the four living creatures and the twenty-four elders fell down before the Lamb. Each one had a harp and they were holding golden bowls full of incense, which are the prayers of the saints. ... The smoke of the incense, together with the prayers of the saints, went up before God from the angel's hand."[c]

A PRAYER LIFE FOLLOWING THE PATTERN OF THE LORD'S PRAYER

The Lord's Prayer, found in Matthew 6, was given to us by Christ as a guide to prayer and how to live our life in a way that pleases him. In this prayer we find the pattern God wants us to have as we pray. The prayer Jesus taught us is,

"And when you pray, do not keep on babbling like pagans, for they think they will be heard because of their many words. Do not be like them, for your Father knows what you need before you ask him. This, then, is how you should pray: "Our Father who art in heaven, hallowed be Thy name. Thy Kingdom come, Thy will be done, on earth as it is in heaven. Give us this day our daily bread and forgive us our trespasses as we forgive those who trespass against us. And lead us not into temptation but deliver us from evil. For Thine is the Kingdom, and the power and the glory forever. Amen."

The pattern of prayer we learn from Jesus in the Lord's Prayer is:

---

[a] Philippians 4:6-7 (NIV)
[b] Matthew 7:7-8
[c] Revelation 5:8, 8:4

81

"When you pray...," Jesus introduces the Lord's Prayer this way as an invitation and to reveal that he expects us to spend time alone with God in prayer every day. He loves us and knows what is best for us, therefore he gave us prayer as a primary means of grace that helps us build and maintain a close relationship with God!

A great idea is to find a place in, or outside, your home where you can daily spend some time with Jesus in prayer and in reading the Bible. Having a special place where you can be alone tells Christ and your family that it is important to you to spend time with him.

"do not keep on babbling ...." With this statement Jesus teaches us that when we pray, we are not to repeat the same things over and over, and we are not to spend a lot of time praying for what we think we need. God knows exactly what we need, and he expects us to trust him to take care of us as we obey him and live in a way that pleases him.

"Our Father who art in heaven, hallowed be Thy name." The prayer starts by calling God 'Father' to remind us of the awesome truth that we have a God who is a perfect, loving, merciful, caring Father, and so much more! We can trust him and tell him everything in our lives; including what we are concerned about, troubled over now or in our past, what we are ashamed about, and thank him for the blessings he has given us.

Then, it reminds us to remember that God is to be 'hallowed.' Hallowed means that God is a holy God who will not allow anything that is not holy into the Kingdom of God. Therefore, he is always working in our lives to transform us into people who love him more than anything else, and to prove it through everything we think, say, and do.

God does all of this because he is a loving Father who wants the absolute best for us!

"Thy Kingdom come, Thy will be done, on earth as it is in heaven." Next, we pray that the Holy Spirit would be in total control of our heart and mind, and that we would live for the glory of God. Then, we ask that God would work through us and our church to bring people to faith in Christ, help them grow in their faith, and to make the world a better place through ministry in the church and world.

"Give us this day our daily bread." Now that our hearts are focused on God and his purposes, we turn to prayers that focus on ourselves. But our prayers are not for selfish things! We are to pray that God would provide all we need TODAY, so that we can faithfully live the kind of life he created us to live.

"forgive us our trespasses as we forgive those who trespass against us." This is to pray for something extremely near and dear to the heart of God: good, caring, loving relationships in our family, our church, and with our friends. Jesus always wants us to remember that he died on the cross so that our sins could be forgiven. Because of this he expects us to always forgive others no matter what they have said or done. If we are not willing to forgive others, then we are telling God we do not want him to forgive us!

"and lead us not into temptation but deliver us from evil." As we grow in our relationship and love for Christ, and follow him, our own sin patterns will rise-up to distract us. Satan will oppose us; he will try to keep us from loving and following Christ. God will allow this because we need to be constantly reminded that we need him! We cannot live a life as a Christian on our own, we need God and his wisdom! So, we must always stay close to Christ and seek and ask for his help and strength to do what pleases him, and not what we might feel like thinking, saying, or doing.

"For Thine is the Kingdom, and the power and the glory forever. Amen." When we end our prayers this way, we are saying to God that all of creation, even our own life, are all about him. God is at the center of everything, and we worship him. God is the only one who has all the power needed to build his Kingdom in our lives and in the world. Life truly is all about God and for his glory!

SOME IDEAS I USE IN MY PRAYER LIFE

In this section I will share some of the lessons I have learned in my times of prayer that have blessed me. Some of what I learned come from scripture, some come from God as I prayed, and some have come from what I have learned from others who are deeper in their walk with Christ.

Focus on Thanksgiving and Praise

When we begin our time with the Lord it is important to take some time to enter his presence. God created us for himself and wants us to come before him to enjoy him and be blessed by our time with him. Our deepest desire truly is to be with our Creator and Savior, so when we take time to be with him the desires and demands of this world fade away, and we can simply rest in his presence. This happens when we,

> "But the LORD is in his holy temple; let all the earth keep silence before him."[a]

> "Enter His gates with thanksgiving and His courts with praise; give thanks to him and praise His name."[b]

"Keep silent before him"

Begin by spending some time in silence before the Lord. Do not think of the things of this world, all the busy things you need to do, the things you need prayer for yourself or others, or questions you have for God. Just spend some time in his presence thinking of nothing else except God.

"Enter His gates with thanksgiving"

Make a list or think of some things of which you are thankful. Then simply thank God for his blessing.

"And His courts with praise"

As we begin to thank God for all he has given, and done for us, our minds should begin moving toward praising God for who he is. Using scripture can help us move from thanks to praise as we focus on who God is and praise him. Many scriptures tell us of the qualities or characteristics of God, use these scriptures to praise him for being the source of all that we have. For example:

> "I love you, O Lord, my strength. The Lord is my rock, my fortress and my deliverer; my God is my rock, in whom I take refuge. He is my shield and the horn of my salvation, my stronghold."[c]

> "Every good thing given, and every perfect gift is from above, coming down from the Father of lights, with whom

---

[a] Habakkuk 2:20 (NAS)
[b] Psalm 100:4
[c] Psalm 18:1-2

there is no variation or shifting shadow."[a]

"The one who does not love does not know God, for God is love."[b]

"Come to Me, all you who labor and are heavy laden, and I will give you rest. Take My yoke upon you and learn from Me, for I am gentle and lowly in heart, and you will find rest for your souls. For My yoke is easy and My burden is light."[c]

Here are a few suggestions that will help you begin your daily time in God's presence. The Psalms are more than praises to God; they are filled with wonder, exultation, anguish, joy, and much more! Read the Psalms out loud as an act of worship, you can even take a Psalm and write it in your own words making it personal. As we focus on thanking and praising God, we truly enter his presence and are ready to hear from him and talk with him.

O. Hallesby said, "To give thanks means to give God glory with our lives, with the wonderful things that happen and how he works within us." God says this through Paul who writes,

"Therefore I urge you, brethren, by the mercies of God, to present your bodies a living and holy sacrifice, acceptable to God, which is your spiritual service of worship."[d]

Spend Time in Confession, Repentance, and Forgiveness

God wants us to come before him with a pure and clean heart. In the Beatitudes in Matthew 5 Jesus says, "Blessed are the pure in heart, for they will see God." God wants our hearts pure because only then can we have true peace with him and others. For this to happen we must be open to admitting the truth to God about ourselves and listening for what he wants to reveal to us about ourselves. If we want to be pure of heart before God, we must understand temptation and how to fight it, humbly practice confession and repentance, and receive and give forgiveness.

Psalm 139 is a great Psalm that declares in verses 1-17 the

---

[a] James 1:17
[b] 1 John 4:8
[c] Matthew 11:28-30
[d] Romans 12:1

wonder of being created by God, and how he watches over us in love wherever we are. The Psalm ends with the Psalmist declaring in the last two verses how he wants God to draw him close so that he will always love God for all that he has done for him, and never become like those who despise him. Those two verses are a great guide to use during your time of confession, repentance, and forgiveness, and to declare your desire to have God draw you close to him. And, to keep you on the path of developing a pure heart as you go on your journey through life. The last two verses are:

- "Search me, O God, and know my heart," . . .
- "test me and know my anxious thoughts." . . .
- "See if there is any offensive way in me," . . .
- "and lead me in the way everlasting." . . .

After each phrase stop and listen for what God might be saying to you. If you are a person who likes to keep a spiritual journal you might try writing down what comes to mind after each phrase. When you are finished with your time of confession remind yourself that God, who cannot lie, tells us that he is faithful and forgives us and cleanses us when we confess our sins to him, as he says in the book of 1 John.

> "If we say that we have no sin, we are deceiving ourselves and the truth is not in us. If we confess our sins, He is faithful and righteous to forgive us our sins and to cleanse us from all unrighteousness."[a]

Understanding Temptation and How to Fight It

Often in life all of us are tempted and it is a struggle to see it, resist it, and overcome it. The wonderful news is that Jesus gives us the way to resist temptation! In his book on temptation Dietrich Bonhoeffer does a masterful job of describing temptation and how to fight it.[12] He discusses the temptations of our fallen passions,[b]

---

[a] 1 John 1:8–9

[b] Our 'fallen passions' were described as our 'sin nature' in chapter two and often are called the 'flesh' or 'lust' in the Bible, all are essential the same. The fallen passions are desires that we have that we put *above our desire and love for God*. Some can be exceptionally good such and family or the beauty of nature. Some can be used for

suffering, pride, and despair, and how to overcome them. In summary of what he stated, it is presumed that we overcome temptation by following the example of Jesus' life, especially the time in the Garden of Gethsemane when he prayed.

During his temptation in the wilderness Jesus showed us how to fight and overcome it.[a] When he was tempted Jesus did not argue or debate with the devil! He simply said after each temptation, "It is written," using scripture! In the last temptation he simply said, "Go, Satan! For it is written, 'you shall worship the Lord your God and serve him only.' Then the devil left him; and behold, angels came and begin to minister to him."

In the Garden of Eden Adam and Eve did not do this when they were tempted by Satan. Instead of simply obeying God, they decided to listen to the tempter and were therefore deceived. Knowing and obeying God's word gives us all that is needed to resist temptation and walk in holiness of life and heart. Resisting temptation with the word of God causes Satan to flee along with the temptation!

Humbly Practicing Confession and Repentance

King David was a man after God's own heart, but he caved into temptation and tried to cover it up.[b] David's confession before God gives us a pattern for confessing our sin.[c] In this Psalm we see David: confessing his sin, speaking the truth about God, asking God to change his heart to restore him, and stating what he will do because of God's love and forgiveness. David's confession is a great example for all of us as we seek to be people after God's own heart. This Psalm is a great one to read often and to follow!

In the book of Luke Jesus tells a story about confession and repentance. The story is about a son who dishonors his father,

---

good or evil such as ambition, fame, power, or money. Some are simply evil such as vanity, revenge, or the ungodly use of sexual desires. We can use them for good or with the help of the Holy Spirit of God fight against them, but for all of them *our desire and love for God must be greater!*

[a] Matthew 4:1-11, Mark 1:12-13, Luke 4:1-13
[b] 1 Kings 3:6, 9:4, 11:4
[c] see Psalm 51

suffers the consequences, eventually comes to his senses, and has his eyes opened. Suddenly, he realizes how much he has sinned! But the story does not end there. It has a great ending of receiving forgiveness and so much more![a]

Receiving and Giving Forgiveness

The son's story continues when he realizes how much his father truly does love him and how he received much more from the father than he deserved. The father sees the young man coming up the road, runs to him, puts his arms around him, and welcomes him back as his son!

If there are times when you are having trouble sensing that God has forgiven you read the story of the prodigal son and his caving into temptation and having his eyes opened. Then, envision yourself in the place of the sinner confessing and returning to his father and receiving forgiveness and blessings. This great story reveals to us the heart of God and his desire to forgive us and bless us! This story told by Jesus is about how much God the Father loves us! He loves us so much that he would forgive everything we have ever done and welcomes us into his Kingdom when we come to Christ!

Temptation, Confession, Repentance, and Forgiveness

After following Jesus for three years during which the Spirit of God revealed to him that Jesus was the Son of God, Peter faced a great temptation. Peter's response gives us insight into how God calls us to respond whenever we are tempted.[b]

In this tragic, and yet, wonderful story we see Peter facing the reality of what it means to utterly understand that Jesus is the Christ, the Son of God, and what it means to follow him when we are tempted. In a deeper way he begins to understand that he does not really know who Jesus is, and what it means to follow him. When he is tempted, and his fallen flesh rises-up, he thinks of self first and what the consequence of following Christ means. And fear rises-up! If we are honest, it can cause fear in us when we

---

[a] Luke 15:11-24

[b] You can read about this wonderful event in the following Scriptures: John 18:15-27, Luke 22:54-62, and John 21:1-19. Be sure to read then in the order shown!

consider the cost of following Christ!

A few moments after he is tempted Peter, begins to understand what he has done. During his darkest hours, as Jesus is led out from a show trial, he looks at one of his best friends and says nothing; a look that said everything! At that moment Peter seems to begin to realize what it means to die to self and live for Christ. He then goes out and weeps over what he has done; he truly confesses what he has done to Christ!

However, the story does not end here! Was Peter truly repentant and forgiven? He was! Because, three days later Peter takes a walk with the risen Christ and understands that his repentance and confession was accepted! How does he know? Because Jesus offers him a new life as a leader in the church!

It is important to understand that to fall into temptation is first a sin toward God carried out in our action toward someone else. Therefore, it is important to first confess all sins to God, what our sin has done to him. Then, carry out the action of confessing to the person hurt and asking for their forgiveness. This pleases God so much because in so many ways forgiveness leads to reconciliation between us and God and with each other, which is the reason Jesus Christ died for us!

When he died Jesus simply and very profoundly said, "'It is finished!' And He bowed His head and gave up His spirit."[a] What Jesus was saying is that all the Father sent him to do was completed. So now we can pray with Thomas à Kempis, "With humble voice, I especially praise and honor you for being so tightly bound to that hard and cold pillar to free us from the chains of our sins and to restore everlasting freedom to us."[13]

The Morning Prayer from the Book of Common Prayer is one of the ways to ask God for forgiveness, "Most merciful God, we confess that we have sinned against you in thought, word, and deed, by what we have done, and by what we have left undone. We have not loved you with our whole heart; we have not loved our neighbors as ourselves. We are truly sorry and we humbly repent. For the sake of your Son Jesus Christ, have mercy on us and forgive us; that we may delight in your will, and walk in your ways, to the glory of your name. Amen.

---

[a] John 19:30 (NAS)

89

May Almighty God have mercy on us, forgive us our sins, through Jesus Christ our Lord, and strengthen us to live in the power of the Holy Spirit, all our days. Amen."

> "The Lord is merciful and gracious,
> slow to anger and abounding in steadfast love.
> He will not always chide,
> nor will he keep his anger forever.
> He does not deal with us according to our sins,
> nor repay us according to our iniquities.
> For as high as the heavens are above the earth,
> so great is his steadfast love toward those who fear him;
> as far as the east is from the west,
> so far does he remove our transgressions from us.
> As a father shows compassion to his children,
> so the Lord shows compassion to those who fear him.
> For he knows our frame;
> he remembers that we are dust."[a]

When you have finished your time of confession, repentance, and forgiveness, rededicate yourself to God through the words of Paul,

> "Therefore, I urge you, brothers, in view of God's mercy, to offer your bodies as living sacrifices, holy and pleasing to God—this is your spiritual act of worship. Do not conform any longer to the pattern of this world, but be transformed by the renewing of your mind. Then you will be able to test and approve what God's will is—his good, pleasing and perfect will."[b]

Intercession - Praying for Others

To 'intercede' is to intervene on behalf of another, therefore, intercessory prayer is the act of praying to God on behalf of others. When instructing Timothy about praying for others Paul wrote,

> "I urge, then, first of all, that requests, prayers, intercession and thanksgiving be made for everyone— for kings and all

---

[a] Psalm 103:8-14 (ESV)
[b] Romans 12:1-2 (NIV)

those in authority, that we may live peaceful and quiet lives in all godliness and holiness."[a]

When praying for others, which is an amazing gift and blessing God has given to us, it is important not to assume that we know what we are to pray. Seeking God's desire for this person and understanding what he wants to accomplish in and through them in the situation is how the prayer should be directed. As Joni Erickson Tada, a well know Christian speaker and author who became a quadriplegic from a diving accident, says, "God permits what he hates, to accomplish what he loves." Her worldwide ministry to handicapped people since her accident is amazing, and certainly shows the truth of her statement and the power of God working through a person fully surrendered to him.

As we pray for someone it is important to first ask God to give us wisdom as to how to pray. Only God knows what he desires to accomplish in their lives, and he gives us the privilege of, under the guidance of the Holy Spirit, helping them discover what his purposes are for them. Therefore, as you are praying for someone keep the following possibilities in mind as you seek God's desires for them.

God's First Priority

As we pray for others keep in mind God's priority for all people is that they come to faith in Christ and mature in their faith to become more Christ-like in character and actions; that, as I said in the introduction, 'they are fit for heaven.' The following verses give us great insight into this ultimate purpose God has for our lives:

"for the Son of Man has come to seek and to save that which was lost."[b]

"For those whom he foreknew he also predestined to be conformed to the image of His Son, in order that he might be the firstborn among many brothers."[c]

"even as He chose us in Him before the foundation of the

---

[a] 1Timothy 2:1-2 (NIV)
[b] Luke 19:10 (NAS)
[c] Romans 8:29

world, that we should be holy and blameless before Him."[a]

"By this we know that we are in Him: the one who says he abides in Him ought himself to walk in the same manner as He walked."[b]

Restoring of Broken Relationships or Repentance

When praying for others it may become clear that the person needs to restore a broken relationship, or repent of something, as the following Scriptures tell us we must do.

"And forgive us our debts, as we also have forgiven our debtors. And do not lead us into temptation, but deliver us from evil. For if you forgive others for their transgressions, your heavenly Father will also forgive you. But if you do not forgive others, then your Father will not forgive your transgressions."[c]

"My heavenly Father will also do the same to you, if each of you does not forgive His brother from your heart."[d]

"Be kind to one another, tender-hearted, forgiving each other, just as God in Christ also has forgiven you."[e]

"In the same way, I tell you, there is joy in the presence of the angels of God over one sinner who repents."[f]

Healing of Some Kind

There can be times when someone, through no fault of their own, goes through a difficult time such as an illness, the death of a loved one, the loss of a job, or a catastrophe of some kind, that God wants to use their Christ-like response as a witness for Christ. Or it may be that God wants to heal them of a hurt in their life that was caused by a traumatic incident that keeps them captive. The following Scriptures can be used by God to bless, comfort, give them hope, or heal them.

A great example from Scripture is seen in the life of a

---

[a] Ephesians 1:4
[b] 1 John 2:5-6
[c] Matthew 6:12–15
[d] Matthew 18:35
[e] Ephesians 4:32
[f] Luke 15:10

righteous man named Job who suffers so much and yet responded by saying,

"Naked I came from my mother's womb, and naked I shall return there. The Lord gave and the Lord has taken away. Blessed be the name of the Lord. Through all this Job did not sin nor did he blame God."[a]

"The Spirit of the Lord God is upon me, because the Lord has anointed me to bring good news to the afflicted; he has sent me to bind up the brokenhearted, to proclaim liberty to captives and freedom to prisoners; to proclaim the favorable year of the Lord and the day of vengeance of our God; to comfort all who mourn, to grant those who mourn in Zion, giving them a garland instead of ashes, the oil of gladness instead of mourning, the mantle of praise instead of a spirit of fainting. So they will be called oaks of righteousness, the planting of the Lord, that he may be glorified."[b]

"He heals the brokenhearted and binds up their wounds."[c]

"The sacrifices of God are a broken spirit; a broken and a contrite heart, O God, You will not despise."[d]

Keep in Mind God's Love for Them

Lastly, always keep in mind that God loves the person you are praying for and always wants the best for them. Praying for others can be transforming for the one offering prayer! As the following Scripture declares, Jesus truly is everyone's best friend!

Psalm 146

Praise the Lord!
Praise the Lord, O my soul!
I will praise the Lord while I live;
I will sing praises to my God while I have my being.
Do not trust in princes,
In mortal man, in whom there is no salvation.

---

[a] Job 1:13-22
[b] Isaiah 61:1–3 (ESV). This Scripture was filled by Jesus as seen in Luke 4:18-19
[c] Psalm 147:3
[d] Psalm 51:17

His spirit departs, he returns to the earth;
In that very day his thoughts perish.
How blessed is he whose help is the God of Jacob,
Whose hope is in the Lord his God,
Who made heaven and earth,
The sea and all that is in them;
Who keeps faith forever;
Who executes justice for the oppressed;
Who gives food to the hungry.
The Lord sets the prisoners free.
The Lord opens the eyes of the blind;
The Lord raises up those who are bowed down;
The Lord loves the righteous;
The Lord protects the strangers;
He supports the fatherless and the widow,
But He thwarts the way of the wicked.
The Lord will reign forever,
Your God, O Zion, to all generations.
Praise the Lord! (NAS)

Praying for Yourself as You Live in a Fallen World

All of us have many concerns in our lives in which we need God's wisdom, love, strength, healing, and perseverance as we live our lives in a fallen world. Since this is obviously true, you can use the suggestion in <u>Intercession - Praying for Others</u> above and make it personal to your circumstance. Also, it is imperative that a daily prayer habit is in our life. Therefore, you are encouraged to use any of the suggestions in this chapter to help you in developing a prayer life.

Throughout your life in whatever circumstances, you find yourself in, remember to …

"Rejoice in the Lord always; again I will say, rejoice! Let your gentle spirit be known to all men. The Lord is near. Be anxious for nothing, but in everything by prayer and supplication with thanksgiving let your requests be made known to God. And the peace of God, which surpasses all comprehension, will guard your hearts and your minds in Christ Jesus. Finally, brethren, whatever is true, whatever is honorable, whatever is right, whatever is pure, whatever is lovely, whatever is of good repute, if there is any excellence and if anything worthy of praise, dwell on these things."[a]

And to,

"Trust in the LORD with all your heart and do not lean on your own understanding. In all your ways acknowledge Him, and he will make your paths straight."[b]

And Never Forget!

God *never* leaves us! However, there are times that it may *seem* he does. So, where is God when I need him most? We must always remember that during his life in the world Jesus felt so much of what we face such as: the grief of a loved one's death, the heartbreak of a close friend's betrayal, and the pain of, perhaps, one day suffering torture and death and saying deep within the soul, "My God, why have you forsaken me?"[c]

But, as we all know, God did not desert Jesus! His Father loved him and was always there with him! We know this is true because three days after his death in God's power, Jesus rose from the grave, conquering death, making it possible for us to have real life with God now and for eternity!

And since Jesus and the Father are One, we know that God is always with those who are his children, because Jesus promised us that he,

"I will ask the Father, and He will give you another Helper, that He may be with you forever; that is the Spirit of truth, whom the world cannot receive, because it does not see Him or know Him, but you know Him because He abides with you and will be in you. "I will not leave you as orphans; I will come to you."[d]

---

[a] Philippians 4:4–8
[b] Proverbs 3:5–6
[c] Matthew 27:46
[d] John 14:16–18, see also Joshua 1:5-9, Hebrews 13:5, 8

95

A PRAYER LIFE BASED ON THE MORNING AND
EVENING PRAYER

The *Morning and Evening Prayer* is a daily devotional that has been used in public and private settings for centuries. When it is used daily (or as often as possible) it provides a structured way of doing daily prayer, and provides a daily reading of the Psalms, Old Testament, New Testament, and the Gospel.

In speaking about morning prayer Dietrich Bonhoeffer says in his book *Psalms: The Prayer Book of the Bible,*

> The entire day receives order and discipline when it acquires unity. This unity must be sought and found in morning prayer. It is confirmed in work. The morning prayer determines the day. Squandered time of which we are ashamed, temptations to which we succumb, weaknesses and lack of courage in work, disorganization and lack of discipline in our thoughts and in our conversation with other men, all have their origin most often in the neglect of morning prayer.[14]

A copy of the *Morning Prayer* is in the Appendix. The apps *Daily Office* and *My Daily Office* are worth using because they make daily changes to the following sections of the devotional: the opening verse, the daily scriptures, The Benediction, etc. If you would like a copy, you can order the *Field Guide for Daily Prayer* from Seedbed.com.

Reading, Meditating On, and Studying the Bible Daily

As followers of Christ, it is vital to read, meditate on, and study the Bible. The Bible is God's Word, and it is the primary source for knowing about God and how we are to follow Christ in the power of the Holy Spirit. As we read the Bible we should pray, "Teach me Your way, O Lord; I will walk in Your truth; Unite my heart to fear Your name."[a]

The Bible says this about itself:

---

[a] Psalm 86:11 (NAS)

"All Scripture is God-breathed and is useful for teaching, rebuking, correcting and training in righteousness, so that the man of God may be thoroughly equipped for every good work."[a]

"For the word of God is living and active. Sharper than any double-edged sword, it penetrates even to dividing soul and spirit, joints and marrow; it judges the thoughts and attitudes of the heart."[b]

"Your word is a lamp to my feet and a light for my path." [c]

"The law of the LORD is perfect, reviving the soul. The statutes of the LORD are trustworthy, making wise the simple. The precepts of the LORD are right, giving joy to the heart. The commands of the LORD are radiant, giving light to the eyes. The fear of the LORD is pure, enduring forever. The ordinances of the LORD are sure and altogether righteous. They are more precious than gold, than much pure gold; they are sweeter than honey, than honey from the comb. By them is your servant warned; in keeping them there is great reward."[d]

"This book of the law shall not depart from your mouth, but you shall meditate on it day and night, so that you may be careful to do according to all that is written in it; for then you will make your way prosperous, and then you will have success."[e]

"But his delight is in the law of the LORD, and in His law he meditates day and night. He will be like a tree firmly planted by streams of water, which yields its fruit in its season and its leaf does not wither; and in whatever he does, he prospers."[f]

"like newborn babies, long for the pure milk of the word, so that by it you may grow in respect to salvation, if you have

---

[a] 2 Timothy 3:16-17
[b] Hebrews 4:12 (NIV)
[c] Psalm 119:105, all of Psalm 119 speaks of having a passion for and living the life God has created us for.
[d] Psalm 19:7-11
[e] Joshua 1:8 (NAS)
[f] Psalm 1:2-3

tasted the kindness of the Lord."[a]

Read again the quote, already mentioned above, from John Wesley with an emphasis on his view of scripture,

> "I have thought, I am a creature of a day, passing through life as an arrow through the air. I am a spirit come from God and returning to God; just hovering over this great gulf till in a few moments hence, I am no more seen, I drop into an unchangeable eternity! I want to know one thing, the way to heaven; how to land safe on that happy shore. God himself has condescended to teach the way, for this very end he came from heaven. He has written it down in a book. O give me that book! At any price give me the book of God! I have it; here is knowledge enough for me. Let me be a man of one book. Here then I am, far from the busy ways of men. I sit down alone. Only God is here. In His presence I open it, I read His book, for this end, to find the way to heaven."[15]

The Bible is not an end but is a means to the end of knowing God, being transformed by him, and doing his will. The apostle Paul said,

> "Be diligent to present yourself approved to God as a workman who does not need to be ashamed, handling accurately the word of truth".[b]

God has given us the Bible in order that we might know him, what his will is for our lives, how to fulfill his purposes here on earth, and be prepared for eternity in paradise with him. As Robert Mulholland Jr. says in "Shaped by The Word," "God's address is usually very pointed, very personal, very practical. It addresses the deep dynamics of our being and doing."[16] Therefore, *always remember that as you study scripture the primary purpose is not knowledge, which is important, but transformation.*

Also, the Bible is one unified book and takes us from creation to rebellion, to salvation, and then restoration. All of it points to Jesus Christ and what he accomplished through his birth, his life, his teachings, his miracles, and ultimately through his

---

[a] 1 Peter 2:2–3
[b] 2 Timothy 2:15

Crucifixion, Resurrection, and Ascension. Keep this in mind while reading and studying the Bible, it truly is written by God to guide us to salvation! Therefore, pray and ask the Holy Spirit for change as you study and meditate on scripture.

Since studying, meditating on and understanding scripture is vital to a growing faith, it is important to have a method that helps in studying the Bible, understand what it means, and learn how to apply it to your life. What follows are some suggestions on doing just that.

Devotional Bible study is one form of Bible study that God can use to fulfill his purposes for our lives. *Devotional Bible study means reading and studying the Word of God in order that we may hear God's voice, that we may know how to do his will, and how to live a godly Christian life.*

For your devotional reading and study of the Bible, here are several important, practical suggestions:

1. Begin your Bible reading with prayer.[a]
2. Read slowly through the entire book you are studying asking yourself this question; What seems to be the overall theme or message of the book?
3. Then, slowly read one chapter, or perhaps two or three chapters, or perhaps just one paragraph or section at a time. After reading, ask yourself what this passage means and how it relates to the overall theme or message of the book. Then read it again.
4. As you read each verse take the time to focus on what that verse says, meditate on it, and then write it in your own words. This truly lets God know you are serious about knowing his Word. If it takes an entire week to do one chapter that is fine. Learning and transformation are the goals, not quantity. To meditate on scripture means to actively interact with the scripture asking what it means, how does it apply to me, etc.
5. It is often extremely helpful in finding out the true meaning of a chapter or passage to ask the following questions, and then write the answers in a notebook. Not all these questions may be answered in every passage.
   • Ask the Holy Spirit to guide you in understanding the

---

[a] Psalm 119:18; John 16:13-15

meaning of the text to the original readers, and how that meaning applies today.

- Look at the stories or teaching before and after the section you are reading to discover deeper spiritual truths.
- What is the main subject of this passage?
- What is the key verse of this passage?
- What does this passage teach me about the Lord Jesus Christ?
- Does this passage reveal any sin for me to confess and turn away from?
- Does it provide comfort in an area where I am hurting?
- Does it give me guidance in an area where I need help?
- Does this passage contain any command or instruction for me to obey?
- Does it speak to me about a ministry God is calling me to in the church or world?
- Is there any promise for me to claim?
- What does it say to me about my relationship with God and others?
- What does it say to me about my priorities?

6. Keep a spiritual diary and daily write down what you think God is saying to you through the Bible.

How George Mueller entered a 'Heart' Relationship with God through: Prayer, Reading and Meditating on the Bible, and the Actions that flowed from them.

George Mueller was a wonderful man of God who in 19th century England built orphanages that ministered to thousands of street children and children in workhouses. He housed them, fed them, clothed them, and taught the skills they needed to be employed. Most importantly, he taught them about Christ and how to follow him. He spent tens of millions of dollars doing this and never asked anyone for funds. God accomplished this through him because he listened to and followed God using the following method.

HOW TO ASCERTAIN THE WILL OF GOD

1. I seek at the beginning to get my heart into such a state that it has no will of its own in regard to a given matter.

100

Nine-tenths of the trouble with people, generally, is just here. Nine-tenths of the difficulties are overcome when our hearts are ready to do the Lord's will, whatever it may be. When one is truly in this state, it is, usually, but a little way to the knowledge of what His will is.

2. Having done this, I do not leave the result to feeling or simple impression. If so, I make myself liable to great delusions.

3. I seek the Will of the Spirit of God through, or in connection with, the Word of God. The Spirit and the Word must be combined. If I look to the Spirit alone without the Word, I lay myself open to great delusions also. If the Holy Ghost guides us at all, He will do it according to the scriptures and never contrary to them.

4. Next, I take into account providential circumstances. These often plainly indicate God's Will in connection with His Word and Spirit.

5. I ask God in prayer to reveal His Will to me aright.

6. Thus, through prayer to God, the study of the Word, and reflection, I come to a deliberate judgment according to the best of my ability and knowledge, and if my mind is thus at peace, and continues so after two or three more petitions, I proceed accordingly. In trivial matters, or in transactions involving most important issues, I have found this method always effective.[17]

May God in his mercy and grace give us people like George Mueller who led us in every area of our culture, as they are guided by God through prayer and the Word of God, and then follow the ways of God as they are led by the Holy Spirit! This prayer from the Common Book of Prayer is used on the second Sunday of Advent and speaks to the heart of scripture.

"Blessed Lord, who caused all holy Scriptures to be written for our learning: Grant us so to hear them, read, mark, learn, and inwardly digest them, that by patience and the comfort of your holy Word we may embrace and ever hold fast the blessed hope of everlasting life, which you have given us in our Savior Jesus Christ; who lives and reigns with you and the Holy Spirit, one God, for ever and ever. Amen."

Worshiping at Least Weekly with Other Christians

As Christians we are part of the Church, the Body of Christ in the world. It is vital to our spiritual growth and salvation that we grow in our faith individually using all the spiritual disciplines in this chapter, *and* that we worship with God's people at least weekly. Together we experience God through song, prayer, hearing God's Word, and the sacraments. God has told us to do this in Bible verses such as,

> "On the first day of the week, when we were gathered together to break bread,"[a]

> "Ascribe to the Lord the glory due His name. Bring an offering and come before him; worship the Lord in the splendor of His holiness."[b]

> "I rejoiced with those who said to me, 'Let us go to the house of the LORD.'"[c]

> "Yet a time is coming and has now come when the true worshipers will worship the Father in spirit and truth, for they are the kind of worshipers the Father seeks. God is spirit, and his worshipers must worship in spirit and in truth."[d]

Often people say they do not go to church because it is boring, they do not get anything out of it, etc. However, *that is not the point of going to a worships service!* We go to church to worship God with the people of God, together we thank him for all he has done for us, to thank him for saving us, for guiding us, and for making it possible for us to spend eternity in heaven – *it is about God, not us!* If this is your attitude you will be blessed! So, make it a perpetual practice to worship at least weekly with the people of God.

---

[a] Acts 20:7
[b] 1 Chronicles 16:29
[c] Psalm 122:1 (NIV)
[d] John 4:23-24

Developing Deep Relationships with Other Christians

The relationships God expects us to have with each other, as Christians, is described in the fifty or more 'one another' verses in the New Testament. A few of them are:

"But encourage one another day after day, as long as it is still called 'Today,' so that none of you will be hardened by the deceitfulness of sin."[a]

"and let us consider how to stimulate one another to love and good deeds, not forsaking our own assembling together, as is the habit of some, but encouraging one another; and all the more as you see the day drawing near."[b]

"Bear one another's burdens, and thereby fulfill the law of Christ."[c]

"Be kind to one another, tender-hearted, forgiving each other, just as God in Christ also has forgiven you."[d]

A summary of these 'one another' verses that describe the life Christians are to live with each other might look something like this:

Christian fellowship is an expression of genuine love freely shared among the members of God's family. It is sharing with others things such as: words of encouragement, confessions of failure, statements of need, and sharing of resources to meet everyone's needs. It is also sharing in something with others such as sorrow, joy, or an area of mutual concern. Fellowship is where true love seeks the greatest good of the other in an atmosphere of genuine expressions of honesty and humility. It is where Christian brothers and sisters lovingly help steer back on course those who fail in seeking to follow Christ rather than judge and reject them. In this atmosphere of true love people can confess their sins and be assured of the forgiveness of God. It is a place where people encourage each other in their walk with Christ. It is a life together

---

[a] Hebrews 3:13 (NAS)
[b] Hebrews 10:24-25
[c] Galatians 6:2
[d] Ephesians 4:32

that is informal and flexible with the focus on spiritually developing God's people rather than routine and structure. (Adapted from *Koinonia: Authentic Fellowship* by Charles Swindoll)

If we are to experience the kind of relationships God desires for us it is especially important that we develop this kind of lifestyle. It is a vital part of our growth in sanctification and preparation for eternal life. The best way to develop this kind of fellowship with other Christians is to be in a small group that encourages this kind of spiritual growth.

Living the Sermon on the Mount as an Expression of a Genuine Christian Life

A good summary of what the goal of our lives as Christians should be is found in the Sermon on the Mount in Matthew chapters 5-7. These three chapters are Jesus' summary of what it is to live as his follower in the Kingdom of God. The Sermon on the Mount begins with the beatitudes in 5:3-12, of which the first one is, "Blessed are the poor in spirit, for theirs is the kingdom of heaven." In this verse 'poor in spirit' means 'beggar or humble.' It ends with Jesus telling us in 7:24-27 that a wise person is one who builds his house on solid rock which means knowing, loving, and following him as revealed in these few chapters, and all of scripture. *I would encourage you to read and meditate on these three chapters several times in the next few days!*

As a conclusion to this chapter, practicing the disciplines as described in this section throughout our lives we will grow in our relationship with Jesus Christ, *and* our relationships with each other will be transformed. We will be 'working out our salvation,' by developing "the attitude that was in Christ Jesus,' and walking "by the Spirit.' The ancient Irish hymn, "Be Thou My Vision," sums up this section well.

> Be Thou my Vision, O Lord of my heart;
> Naught be all else to me, save that Thou art;
> Thou my best Thought, by day or by night,
> Waking or sleeping, Thy presence my light.
>
> Be Thou my Wisdom, and Thou my true Word;

I ever with Thee and Thou with me, Lord;
Thou my great Father, I Thy true son;
Thou in me dwelling, and I with Thee one.

Riches I heed not, nor man's empty praise,
Thou mine Inheritance, now and always:
Thou and Thou only, first in my heart,
High King of Heaven, my Treasure Thou art.

High King of Heaven, my victory won,
May I reach Heaven's joys, O bright Heav'n's Sun!
Heart of my own heart, whatever befall,
Still be my Vision, O Ruler of all.

Chapter 9

A Journey of Making Marriage and Family a Priority

The biblical truth of marriage and family, as a lifelong covenant relationship between one man and one woman, and the children that are created from this union, flows from the heart of God and is therefore a matter of justice and righteousness. The importance of justice and righteousness cannot be understated when they are applied to marriage and family. Marriage and family are God's foundational building blocks of a culture and when promoted and practiced, as created, and intended by God, produce a stable and peaceful culture where righteousness and justice reigns.

The word 'justice' in the Hebrew language stands for the creating of just laws according to the ways of God that are enforced in the culture. This kind of justice punishes those who are violating the ways and commandments of God and protects those who are victims of injustice. The word 'righteousness' in the Hebrew language stands for each person being ethically right according to the ways of God in their heart and mind, and the actions that flow from them. The importance of justice and righteousness can be seen in these few scriptures:

"Thus says the LORD: 'Let not the wise man boast in his wisdom, let not the mighty man boast in his might, let not the rich man boast in his riches, but let him who boasts boast in this, that he understands and knows me, that I am the LORD who practices steadfast love, justice and righteousness in the earth. For in these things I delight, declares the LORD.'"[a]

"You have a strong arm; Your hand is mighty, Your right hand is exalted. Righteousness and justice are the foundation

---

[a] Jeremiah 9:23-24

106

of Your throne; Lovingkindness and truth go before You."[a]

"Righteousness will go before Him and will make His footsteps into a way."[b]

When I think of each of us being created in the image of God, I believe we see that image reflected beautifully in many ways, especially in God's creation of marriage and family. When God revealed to us that the Godhead is made up of three persons whom we know as Father, Son, and Holy Spirit, we see a reflection of that 'community' of three persons in God's creation of male and female, calling them to come together in marriage as husband and wife, and creating children. Embedded in the beautiful story of Genesis 1 and 2 we see God establishing the primary and foundational relationships of humanity: marriage between one man and one woman, the children that are naturally created in that marriage, and the children who are adopted by the married couple.

Even before the Fall, God created marriage calling Adam and Eve to come together as one when he said, "Therefore a man shall leave His father and His mother and hold fast to His wife, and they shall become one flesh."[c] This definition was reaffirmed by Jesus and by Paul.[d] If righteousness were to continue to be practiced by Adam and Eve; between them and God, between each other, and with the children that resulted from their marriage, then justice would exist on the earth.

If we are to understand marriage and how vitally important it is to a stable and just culture, it is vital to know and believe that the marriage relationship between a husband and a wife represents the relationship between Christ and the church. It should reflect what is seen in Ephesians which says,

"Wives, submit to your husbands as to the Lord. For the husband is the head of the wife as Christ is the head of the church, His body, of which he is the Savior. Now as the church submits to Christ, so also wives should submit to their husbands in everything. Husbands, love your wives, just as

---

[a] Psalm 89:13–14.
[b] Psalm 85:13
[c] Genesis 2:24
[d] Matthew 19:5, Ephesians 5:31

Christ loved the church and gave himself up for her to make her holy, cleansing her by the washing with water through the word, and to present her to himself as a radiant church, without stain or wrinkle or any other blemish, but holy and blameless. In this same way, husband's ought to love their wives as their own bodies. He who loves His wife loves himself. After all, no one ever hated His own body, but he feeds and cares for it, just as Christ does the church— for we are members of His body. 'For this reason, a man will leave His father and mother and be united to His wife, and the two will become one flesh.' This is a profound mystery—but I am talking about Christ and the church. However, each one of you also must love His wife as he loves himself, and the wife must respect her husband."[a]

Reason Number One for Marriage: Unity with God

With this understanding we could say that marriage was created and designed by God not to make husbands and wives happy but to make them holy![b]. As husbands and wives die to self and in love serve each other, each one will grow closer to Christ and emulate his passion in their lives. St. Augustine said, "the sacrament of marriage to one is a symbol that in the future we shall all be united and subject to God in the one heavenly city." Augustine was saying that we are to understand that God's primary purpose in creating marriage was to create a sacrament; something that points beyond itself to Someone greater.

Marriage points to the wonderful truth that when we received Christ we were married to God; he became our Bridegroom, and we became his Bride! In our marriage to God in Christ he made the following promise, "I, Jesus Christ, take you a sinner, to be my bride, to have and to hold from this day forward, for better, for worse, for richer, for poorer, in sickness and in health, to love and to cherish, for all eternity. This is my solemn vow." And we in response said, "I, a sinner, take you Jesus Christ as my Savior and Lord, as my Bridegroom, to have and to hold from this day

---

[a] Ephesians 5:22-33 (EVS)
[b] From *Sacred Marriage* by Gary Thomas

forward, for better, for worse, for richer, for poorer, in sickness and in health, to love and to cherish, for all eternity. This is my solemn vow." These verses in Ephesians, and the marriage vows that are used in the church that are based on them, are given to us by God to reveal to us how God relates to us individually, how we are to relate to one another in marriage, and each other in the Church, which is the Bride of Christ!

Reason Number Two for Marriage: Unity of Husband and Wife

Another reason marriage was created by God is so that the husband and wife can enjoy the benefits relationally and physically of a committed, lifelong friend and partner in life. Woman was created from the side of man for a reason. Through this event God was revealing to us that he wanted us to have a partner, someone to share life with, as together we go on our journey through life helping and encouraging each other to love and follow God into the life he created us to live. In the eyes of God, men and women are different in abilities and gifts, but equal in importance and equal in partnership as each one contributes to a rich life together.

In this partnership men are to be the spiritual leaders. In Adam's failure to lead Eve we see an example of what happens when God's ordained and created ways are violated. The husband has been given by God the role of spiritual leadership in keeping the marriage and the family on the path toward spiritual maturity as lovers and followers of Christ. When a wife sees her husband, and children see their father, humbly loving and following Christ they have a living example that helps them navigate the many struggles and temptations life brings. When a man leads this way, he is fulfilling one of the primary purposes for his creation and establishing the foundation for a strong, stable, loving home. He is practicing righteous living which leads to justice.

Reason Number Three for Marriage: Creating of Children and Leading Them to God

A third reason for the creation of marriage is the creation of a family and the nurturing of the children, biological or through adoption. Children are a reward from God as declared by God when he said, "Behold, children are a gift of the Lord, the fruit of the womb is a reward."[a]

That is why scripture clearly declares God's deep love for children, and the primary purpose of parenting is to give children a secure, safe place to be nurtured, so that they can come to know Christ, and as a result be healthy, productive members of society. Jesus made this clear when he saw children being kept from him and with indignation said,

> "Let the children come to me; do not hinder them, for to such belongs the kingdom of God."[b].

It has been proven many times that the best environment for children is a home with a good marriage so that the children can have the training and nurturing of their mother and father. Therefore, some especially important questions to ask are, "How do we help children come to Christ, and in what ways do we hinder them from doing so?"

The primary age for coming into a saving faith in Christ is childhood; therefore, all of us who are disciples of Christ should make it a primary goal of life to bring ours and all children to faith in Christ. We should make it a high goal of our marriages, families, and churches, to create an environment that brings children to the foot of the cross. This environment our children see and experience should be filled with the peace of Christ nurtured through passionate worship, a love for and practice of personal and group prayer, study and meditation on scripture in private and group studies, loving service to the family of God, and outreach into the community in service, evangelism and discipleship. To fail to do this is to fail at the primary purpose of God in blessing us with children: to bring them to faith in Christ so they may know him, love him, enjoy him, serve him, and spend eternity with him in heaven.

If Jesus has such a deep love for children, it makes sense that scripture would give us some guidance as to how we are to bring our children to Christ? I believe a Scripture found in Deuteronomy is foundational in understanding our God given responsibility and privilege of bringing children to faith in Christ. As you read it look very carefully at the heart, role, and he

---

[a] Psalm 127:3
[b] Mark 10:14

110

lifestyle of parents, and others involved with children. They are to have this at home, in the church, and in the community,

> "Hear, O Israel! The Lord is our God, the Lord is one! You shall love the Lord your God with all your heart and with all your soul and with all your might. These words, which I am commanding you today, shall be on your heart. You shall teach them diligently to your sons and shall talk of them when you sit in your house and when you walk by the way and when you lie down and when you rise up. You shall bind them as a sign on your hand and they shall be as frontals on your forehead. You shall write them on the doorposts of your house and on your gates."[a]

We find a great example of how to disciple our children in Susanne Wesley, the mother of John Wesley, who had ten children and spent one hour a week with each child teaching them the truth of the Bible. If marriage is not between one man and one woman committed to each other for life, how can we obey God and create this spiritual environment for the children, he blesses us with?

The vital importance of the father and mother in the faith development of children is found in scriptures, such as Ephesians, where Paul is instructing fathers and says,

> "Fathers, do not provoke your children to anger, but bring them up in the discipline and instruction of the Lord."[b]

If a father is not present in the home, it makes it exceedingly difficult for him to be actively involved in the development of his children's faith.[c] On David Servant's website there is an article about Family-Style Devotions that can help strengthen the spiritual life of a family, the book 'Family Style Devotions' that can be ordered, and a copy of 147 devotions to use with children that can be downloaded or received by email. As of this writing his website is davidservant.com.

---

[a] Deuteronomy 6:4-9

[b] Ephesians 6:4, read and meditate on the meaning of Psalm 78.
It is a powerful message to all parents, and to all of us!

[c] Please read Genesis 8:19, Exodus 12:26, Deuteronomy 11:19,
Job 15:1, Psalm 78:1-18, Psalm 145:4, Proverbs 22;6, Isaiah 39:19,
Joel 1:3, and Colossians 3:21 to see this vital, revealed truth of God!

Reason Number Four for Marriage: Creating a Strong Culture

Lastly, do you see how this focus on marriage creates a strong culture? Because marriage is to reflect the image of God and the relationship between Christ and the church, a husband and wife will take their vows very seriously and do the hard work of creating a strong marriage. In turn this will create a stable and loving home for children that will help them come to faith in Christ and be mature citizens who contribute to the strength of their culture, a culture where justice and righteousness reigns.

The question is how do we create this strong marriage and family? In *Christian to the Core* the International Leadership Institute says, "God creates people for relationships, and we learn about relationships best within families in common ways."[18] The following six characteristics of strong families, taken from the *Christian to the Core* book, give us a wonderful guide for creating strong, godly families. The subjects relating to family includes: Strong Commitment, Spending Enjoyable Time Together, Good Communication, Appreciation and Affection for Each Other, Ability to Solve Problems and React in Crisis, and Shared Spiritual Life. For more information and to order the book go to christiantothecore.org.

Some Closing Thoughts on Marriage and Family

In closing out this chapter, I believe we can rightfully say that the injustice that we see at every level of our culture can be traced primarily to the failure to create biblical marriages and families. Healthy biblical marriages and families are the primary building blocks of a strong, healthy culture. If marriage and family, as defined this way, are weakened through personal sin or through a culture's attempt to subvert them, deep and painful problems will result. This is inevitable because it goes against the very image of the God of which we were created. Therefore, creating a godly marriage and family should be considered the deepest form of practicing justice and righteousness; a justice and righteousness that spreads out from the family and permeates the culture.

Therefore God, who in love created us in his image, calls us to represent that image in a marriage between one man and one

112

woman in a sexual relationship until they are parted by death. It is why any sexual relationship not found within a marriage between one man and one woman is sin. And therefore abortion is sin because it kills unborn children created in the image of God, rather than raising them up to be a blessing to him, to the people he or she will meet throughout his or her life, and to fulfill the plans God has for them.[a]

God created us in love and therefore knows how we are to live our lives, and he wants to guide us in living the lives we were created to live. That is why everyone who has been responsible for a divorce or an abortion needs to understand that it is sin. It is sin because divorce violates the covenant made in our marriage vows, and abortion kills a child being formed in the image of God while it is still in the mother's womb.

When discussing who is responsible for a divorce or an abortion, we must not be too quick to judge, in fact *we* must not judge at all for only God alone can judge! Often only one partner wants a divorce which causes great pain to the other partner, and to their children. The one who wants the divorce has committed the sin, the other has not sinned but must bear the pain it causes. The same is true about abortion, the mother may not want to abort her child, but the pressures from others who want the abortion may be too much for the mother to overcome. The one who wants the abortion has committed the sin along with the mother, but she must bear the pain it causes.

However, when we are humble and admit our sin to God, he is faithful and just to forgive us and cleanse us of all our sins! He opens his arms of love, healing, and care, and lets us know that we are forgiven! Because of this we can know that we are free from our guilt. Then, God works in our life to bring healing to our hearts and helps us move into the life he created us to live! I invite you to go over once again the sections, Spend Time in Confession and Repentance and Praying for Yourself as You Live in a Fallen World in the chapter "A Journey of Developing a Deep Relationship" with God, as you take this to God in prayer.

This biblical definition of marriage does not mean that all

---

[a] Please read Psalm 139:13-16, Jeremiah 1:5, and Job 10:8 to see this vital, revealed truth of God!

people should be married. Many people are called by God to be single, and very fulfilled and complete in their singleness. Their relationship with Christ, family, friends, and the church can make their lives as deeply fulfilling and rewarding as that of a married person.

In a culture that has perverted freedom into meaning license to do pretty much whatever we want; we must continuously remind ourselves that personal desires and passions cannot be allowed to dictate truth or policy. We are all deeply affected by humanity's rebellion against God and are easily deceived. Therefore, we must always turn to scripture and its meaning as determined throughout the ages of Christianity to determine truth. Christ alone is Truth itself. We are not. So, no matter what we feel or desire, we must humbly bow to Christ and stand firm for and declare the truth of scripture no matter what the cost to self. After all, that is what Christ did and he said, "Follow me."

In Hebrews 11 we find many heroes of the faith who would not settle for what this world offered. Instead, they pursued the unseen kingdom of God with all their hearts. They sought to do all they could in God's strength to do his will in this world but did not expect perfection until the Messiah was fully revealed. We must do the same in sure and certain hope that when Christ returns to set up his perfect Kingdom, we will all be transformed through the removal of the unique imprint our sin nature has on each of us, and the receiving of perfect, sin-free, glorified bodies and souls for eternity. In the meantime, let us do all we can, through the Church and in the power of the Holy Spirit, to bring the reign of Christ into our lives, our marriages, our families, our church, and the world; always looking forward with sure and certain faith, hope, and love that Christ will someday restore all things as they were meant to be.

> "He will wipe away every tear from their eyes; and there will no longer be any death; there will no longer be any mourning, or crying, or pain; the first things have passed away. And He who sits on the throne said, 'Behold, I am making all things new.' And He said, 'Write, for these words are faithful and true.'" Revelation 21:4–5 (NAS)

Chapter 10

A Journey of Faithfully Using all God has Blessed You With

Now, let us look at how God hopes we will use all the blessings he has given us. As you read the following Scripture what does it say about who created all that exists? Who owns it?

"O Lord God Almighty, who is like You? You are mighty, O Lord, and Your faithfulness surrounds You. You rule over the surging sea; when its waves mount up, You still them... The heavens are Yours, and Yours also the earth; You founded the world and all that is in it. You created the north and the south.... Your arm is endued with power; Your hand is strong, Your right hand exalted."[a]

God reveals to us in scripture that he has blessed us with three major gifts, that he expects those who are his children to use wisely: those gifts are finances, time, and spiritual gifts.[b] At the end of our lives as we stand before God, he will expect us to explain how we have used these gifts, and if we have used them wisely, we will hear him say,

"Well done, good and faithful servant! You have been faithful with a few things; I will put you in charge of many things. Come and share your master's happiness!'"[c]

God, who is loving, kind, and all-powerful, created and owns all that exists, even us! Knowing that we will answer to God for the use of all he has blessed us with, should cause us to look at how God expects us to faithfully use them. In the last chapter we looked at how God wants us to be faithful with the blessings of marriage and family. Now let us look at how God calls us to faithfully use other blessings he gives to his people.

---

[a] Psalm 89:8, 12, 13
[b] Matthew 25
[c] Matthew 25:23

115

First, God calls his people to bless him as they support the work of his Kingdom through the church and its ministries.

"Thus all the tithe of the land, of the seed of the land or of the fruit of the tree, is the Lord's; it is holy to the Lord."[a]

Bring the whole tithe into the storehouse, so that there may be food in My house, and test Me now in this,' says the Lord of hosts, 'if I will not open for you the windows of heaven and pour out for you a blessing until it overflows.'"[b]

As children of God, we will step out in faith and move toward giving at least a tenth of our income to building his Kingdom. We can trust him to provide all we need to take care of our families and to accomplish the work he calls us to do.

Next, God expects us to use the rest of our resources wisely and generously. In the book of Luke[c] Jesus told two stories that teach the wisdom of this principle, where he says,

"Give, and it will be given to you. They will pour into your lap a good measure—pressed down, shaken together, and running over. For by your standard of measure it will be measured to you in return." [d]

Jesus is calling us to carefully consider how resources are used at home as a testimony to our family, in the world to bless others, and to glorify him.

In addition, Jesus also calls us to use the time he gives wisely. Jesus knew that his time was limited. In John he makes this clear by saying,

"We must work the works of Him who sent Me as long as it is day; night is coming when no one can work." [e]

Jesus was always aware of the purpose his Father had sent him into the world as seen in the book of John, when he prayed,

"I glorified You on the earth, having accomplished the work

---

[a] Leviticus 27:30
[b] Malachi 3:10
[c] Luke 14:27-33
[d] Luke 6:38
[e] John 9:4

116

which You have given Me to do." [a]

God expects that we will also want to glorify him just as Jesus did. That is why Jesus said,

> "Do you not say, 'Four months more and then the harvest'? I tell you, open your eyes and look at the fields! They are ripe for harvest.'" [b]

It is vital to understand that God does not expect us to do all this on our own! He promised to always be with us, and to equip us with spiritual gifts so that we can live for him! As you read the three Scriptures below look for the source of our spiritual gifts in Romans, the source of the work God has for us in Ephesians, and the ultimate purpose of spiritual gifts in Ephesians 4.

> "Just as each of us has one body with many members, and these members do not all have the same function, so in Christ we who are many form one body, and each member belongs to all the others. We have different gifts, according to the grace given us."[c]

> "For we are God's workmanship, created in Christ Jesus to do good works, which God prepared in advance for us to do."[d]

> "To prepare God's people for works of service, so that the body of Christ may be built up until we all reach unity in the faith and in the knowledge of the Son of God and become mature, attaining to the whole measure of the fullness of Christ. Then we will no longer be infants, tossed back and forth by the waves, and blown here and there by every wind of teaching and by the cunning and craftiness of men in their deceitful scheming. Instead, speaking the truth in love, we will in all things grow up into Him who is the Head, that is, Christ. From Him the whole body, joined and held together by every supporting ligament, grows and builds itself up in love, as each part does its work."[e]

---

[a] John 17:4
[b] John 4:35
[c] Romans 12:46
[d] Ephesians 2:10
[e] Ephesians 4:12-16

God also gives us the blessing of work and expects us to use it wisely. Even before the Fall, which occurred in Genesis 2, God gave us the blessing of work in Genesis 2:15. Work can be outside of the home, in the home, or both, each one is of great importance and both are of equal value, contributing to the creation of a loving home.

Work also makes it possible for us to help other people as in Ephesians which says,

> "He who steals must steal no longer; but rather he must labor, performing with his own hands what is good, so that he will have something to share with one who has need."[a]

Work should be understood as not really working for people but for the Lord, so that we can be a witness to others of what it means to serve God as seen in Colossians,

> "Whatever you do, do your work heartily, as for the Lord rather than for men, knowing that from the Lord you will receive the reward of the inheritance. It is the Lord Christ whom you serve."[b]

We should also work in a quiet and humble attitude so that we can help make the work environment a great place to work for ourselves and for others as seen in 1 Thessalonians,

> "and to make it your ambition to lead a quiet life and attend to your own business and work with your hands, just as we commanded you,"[c]

And finally, God tells us through Paul that those who are able to work should work in order to take care of themselves and not be people who cause problems at home or in the community when he says,

> "For even when we were with you, we used to give you this order: if anyone is not willing to work, then he is not to eat, either. For we hear that some among you are leading an undisciplined life, doing no work at all, but acting like busybodies. Now such persons we command and exhort in

---

[a] Ephesians 4:28
[b] Colossians 3:23–24
[c] 1 Thessalonians 4:11

the Lord Jesus Christ to work in quiet fashion and eat their own bread."[a]

This has been a very brief overview of just a few of the gifts God has blessed us with, and how we are to faithfully use them. Over time you will learn more about these wonderful gifts, and as you learn about and use them wisely your love for God will grow and your desire to use them for his glory will increase.

You may want to use the last two verses of Psalm 139 that were used in the chapter *A Journey of Developing a Deep Relationship with God.* After each phrase stop and listen for what God might be saying to you about how you are to use all the blessings, he has given to you.

Those verses are:

- "Search me, O God, and know my heart," . . .
- "test me and know my anxious thoughts." . . .
- "See if there is any offensive way in me," . . .
- "and lead me in the way everlasting." . . .

Do you have an idea of how God can use your finances, time, and spiritual gifts to bring the Kingdom of God on earth?

---

[a] 2 Thessalonians 3:10–12

Chapter 11

A Journey of Discovering God's Ministry for Your Life

As growth in our relationship with Christ begins, a growing desire to use the gifts and abilities God has given us to serve him will be sensed. Our response to God's call to serve him may be something we never thought of doing, but we can trust him to guide and equip us for it and move into it in love and gratitude for all he has done for us. This service to God will come in the form of a desire to make a difference in the lives of others through serving in the church and in the world. Hopefully, it will help make the world a better place, but the primary motive should be to serve and glorify God, and help others see Christ in our lives and receive him as Savior and Lord.

The following Scriptures reveal God's desire for us to serve him by serving others:

"I tell you the truth, whatever you did for one of the least of these brothers of mine, you did for me."[a]

"Now that I, your Lord and Teacher, have washed your feet, you also should wash one another's feet. I have set you an example that you should do as I have done for you."[b]

"For it is by grace you have been saved, through faith - and this not from yourselves, it is the gift of God - not by works, so that no one can boast. For we are God's workmanship, created in Christ Jesus to do good works, which God prepared in advance for us to do."[c]

"So also faith by itself, if it does not have works, is dead. But someone will say, 'You have faith and I have works.' Show me your faith apart from your works, and I will show you my

---

[a] Matthew 25:40 (NIV)
[b] John 13:14-15
[c] Ephesians 2:8-10

120

faith by my works."[a]

Serving God is what life is all about, as we live within our families, the church, and the world. As the Book of Daily Prayer says, "For the sake of your Son Jesus Christ, have mercy on us and forgive us; that we may delight in your will, and walk in your ways, to the glory of your name."

According to the Bible the very reason for man's creation was to glorify God by knowing him, loving him, and serving him.[b] According to the book of Ecclesiastes we were not created to 'chase the wind' but to join God in his mission to redeem broken people and a broken world.

Throughout the Bible God calls us to love him with all our heart, soul, mind, and strength, and to love our neighbors as ourselves.[c] Instead of being 'religious,' we are to absolutely love God and serve him by caring as deeply for others as we care for ourselves. This is done by learning to know God intimately, witnessing to the lost, and caring passionately for the poor, the powerless, and the oppressed.[d] This mission means to follow the example of Jesus as we "pick up our cross daily and follow him", understanding that Jesus gave us the ultimate example of following the will of his Father by going to the cross to purchase our salvation.[e] And finally, we understand that this often does not just mean family, friends, and neighbors, but this call to mission and prayer can include people, environmental disasters, people under persecution, and other concerns, in our nation and the world.[f]

In Acts God says, "and David served the purposes of God in his generation."[g] The question that must be asked is: "Do I want to just sit by and watch as others are used by God to change the world? Or do I want to receive fulfillment and joy as I join God, under the guidance and power of the Holy Spirit, in building his

---

[a] James 2:17–18 (ESV), Matthew 25 shows importance faith and works
[b] 1 Corinthians 10:31, Romans 10:36, Psalm 73:25-28, Ephesians 2:10
[c] Matthew 22:37-39
[d] Isaiah 58:6-12, Luke 19:10, James 1:27
[e] John 6:38, John 14:9-11, Matthew 26:42, Mark 14:36, Luke 22:42
[f] Matthew 28:18-20
[g] Acts 13:36

Kingdom?" Have you sensed that God has a vision, a purpose, for your life? What is your answer?

WHAT IF I HAVE NO GIFTS?

Many people feel that they do not have anything to offer God, but this is simply not true. Everyone has God-given gifts, natural abilities they were born with, knowledge they have gained, and talents they have developed. Everyone has a God given passion; something that inspires them deep in their heart. All of us have had experiences in our lives that have matured us, pain that has deepened us, and the love of God that is "poured out within our hearts".[a] God has given you a needed special gift, even if you are not aware of it, to accomplish his purposes for you in service to him!

"However, each man has His own gift from God, one in this manner, and another in that."[b]

"As each one has received a special gift, employ it in serving one another as good stewards of the manifold grace of God."[c]

The world's message is: It is all about you. Be happy. Indulge yourself. Fulfill your dreams. This kind of thinking leads us to think, "How can serving help me?" However, if we are honest, deep within ourselves, we know that serving only ourselves does not make us happy, it does not fulfill us. In fact, it leaves us feeling empty. Someone once said, "True fulfillment will never come through self-gratification. It will never lead to the fullness of life you are looking for. And along the way, you will destroy other people."

True Christianity turns the ways of this world upside down. Jesus said,

"If anyone wants to be first, he must be the very last, and the servant of all. If anyone wishes to come after Me, he must deny himself, and take up his cross and follow Me. For whoever wishes to save his life will lose it, but whoever loses

---

[a] Romans 5:5
[b] 1 Corinthians 7:7b (NAS)
[c] 1 Peter 4:10

his life for My sake and the gospel's will save it."[a]

In this passage and in others, Jesus clearly tells us that if we want to be blessed we must choose to make Jesus Christ the center of our lives and become his servants.[b] The book of Philippians[c] tells us Jesus gives us the perfect example through his own life and challenges each of us to decide: will I live a self-centered life, or will I pursue Christ and follow his example by living a life-giving life? Will I be like Jesus who died so that others may live?

DISCOVERING WHERE YOU CAN SERVE

One of the first questions to ask yourself when praying about where to serve is: "What passions do I have for ministry?" When we look at people who make a difference there is a word often used to describe them, PASSION! Mother Teresa had a passion for the poor, and Billy Graham had a passion for the unsaved. These people did well where they served largely because they had a passion for what they did; they loved their work! In the Bible we find great passion in Jesus[d] and John the Baptist.[e] If we are going to serve God well, it is so important to serve where we have a passion, where we find joy in our work.

It is also especially important to realize that as children of God we are called by him to fulfill his purposes. Jesus tells us that purpose when he says,

> "Therefore go and make disciples of all nations, baptizing them in the name of the Father and of the Son and of the Holy Spirit, and teaching them to obey everything I have commanded you. And surely I am with you always, to the very end of the age."[f]

Notice that Jesus said, "I am with you always." Jesus does not expect us to do what he calls us to do alone! He will do it through us! This wonderful truth gives us the courage and strength to

---

[a] Mark 8:34-35
[b] Mark 10:29-31 and John 13:12-17
[c] Philippians 2:3-8
[d] John 14:1
[e] John 3:22-20
[f] Matthew 28:19-20 NIV

follow Jesus. When God calls us, we should respond like Mary did when she was still a virgin, and the angel told her she would be the mother of Jesus,

> "Behold, the bondslave of the Lord; may it be done to me according to your word."[a]

Mother Teresa is a wonderful example of what it means to be a "bondslave of the Lord." Once she said,

> "I'm a little pencil in the hand of a writing God, who is sending a love letter to the world … He does the thinking. He does the writing. He does everything and sometimes it is really hard because it is a broken pencil and He has to sharpen it a little more."

Throughout the ages countless people, like Mary and Mother Theresa, have lived out the words of a Psalm which challenge us by saying,

> "Oh give thanks to the Lord, call upon His name; Make known His deeds among the peoples."[b]

Shouldn't we also live out these words? In the book of Hebrews God tells us,

> "that we may receive mercy and find grace to help in time of need."[c]

Let us end with a prayer from the *Book of Common Prayer*, and then take the time you need to answer an important question. "Most merciful God, we confess that we have sinned against you in thought, word, and deed, by what we have done, and by what we have left undone. We have not loved you with our whole heart; we have not loved our neighbors as ourselves. We are truly sorry and we humbly repent. For the sake of your Son Jesus Christ, have mercy on us and forgive us; that we may delight in your will, and walk in your ways, to the glory of your name.

Almighty God, whose most dear Son went not up to joy but first he suffered pain and entered not into glory before he was crucified: Mercifully grant that we, walking in the way of the

---

[a] Luke 1:38 NAS
[b] Psalm 105:1
[c] Hebrews 4:14-5:6

cross, may find it none other than the way of life and peace; through Jesus Christ our Lord. Amen."

As you pray, study scriptures, and observe the needs of the people of the world, has God put in your heart something he wants to do for his mission on the earth? If you do not sense that God has yet put a mission in your heart, then keep praying and look around you, and God will guide you to what he wants you to do.

A couple of books that may be helpful are: *Experiencing God: Knowing and Doing the Will of God* by Henry T. Blackaby & Claude V. King, and *How Now Shall We Live?* by Charles Colson and Nancy Pearcey.

Chapter 12

A Journey of
Sharing Christ with Others

John Wesley, the founder of Methodism, expressed his passion for sharing Christ with others when he said, "Let us all be of one business. We live only for this, to save our own souls and the souls of those who hear us." His brother Charles wrote of his passion in one of his hymns, "A charge to keep I have, A God to glorify. A never-dying soul to save and fit it for the sky."

There is no doubt that the passion John and Charles felt for those who do not know Christ came from Christ himself and fueled the great Methodist movement of the 18th and 19th centuries in England and America. I can imagine that scriptures, such as this from Matthew, inspired them,

> "Jesus went through all the towns and villages, teaching in their synagogues, preaching the good news of the Kingdom and healing every disease and sickness. When he saw the crowds, he had compassion on them, because they were harassed and helpless, like sheep without a shepherd. Then he said to his disciples, 'The harvest is plentiful but the workers are few. Ask the Lord of the harvest, therefore, to send out workers into His harvest field.'"[a]

As Christians we must develop a passion for the lost and seek an opportunity to share Christ with them. We see this call of Jesus in what is called The Great Commission given by Jesus just before his Ascension into heaven when he said,

> "All authority in heaven and on earth has been given to Me. Therefore go and make disciples of all nations, baptizing them in the name of the Father and of the Son and of the Holy Spirit, and teaching them to obey everything I have commanded you. And surely I am with you always, to the

---

[a] Matthew 9:35-38

very end of the age.'"[a]

Paul wrote the following in the inspired book of Romans about the need for people to share the good news about Jesus Christ when writing,

> "How then will they call on Him in whom they have not believed? How will they believe in Him whom they have not heard? And how will they hear without a preacher? How will they preach unless they are sent? Just as it is written, 'How beautiful are the feet of those who bring good news of good things!'"[b]

When reading the Great Commission did you notice that Jesus calls us to 'baptize' and 'teach'? As we have already seen salvation is not a one-time decision to receive Jesus Christ as Savior; it is an ongoing journey of spiritual transformation into being a person who, as Charles Wesley said above, is 'fit for the sky.'

Now, read the following Scriptures and look for the goal of discipleship and who is to do the work of helping others be 'fit for the sky'.

> "It was he who gave some to be apostles, some to be prophets, some to be evangelists, and some to be pastors and teachers, to prepare God's people for works of service, so that the body of Christ may be built up until we all reach unity in the faith and in the knowledge of the Son of God and become mature, attaining to the whole measure of the fullness of Christ. Then we will no longer be infants, tossed back and forth by the waves, and blown here and there by every wind of teaching and by the cunning and craftiness of men in their deceitful scheming. Instead, speaking the truth in love, we will in all things grow up into Him who is the Head, that is, Christ. From Him the whole body, joined and held together by every supporting ligament, grows and builds itself up in love, as each part does its work."[c]

"And the things you have heard Me say in the presence of

---

[a] Matthew 28:18-20
[b] Romans 10:14-15
[c] Ephesians 4:11-16

many witnesses entrust to reliable men and women who will also be faithful to teach others."[a]

In the above verses from Ephesians and 2 Timothy what is the goal of discipleship? Who is to be involved in helping others reach this goal? When you first thing about sharing the gospel of Christ with others it can be intimidating! But take comfort with the knowledge that God does not expect or call everyone to be an evangelist, pastor, or teacher in the way we commonly think of them. However, God does expect us to live a life that is attractive to other people as we serve them by using the spiritual gifts and the natural talents, he gives us. As we use those gifts and talents in humility and love to help others, they can see that we are different and often will ask what is different about us. When they do ask us, we can share the story of our faith in Christ and then refer them to others who are equipped to teach them about the faith. Hopefully the following will give you some other ideas of how to share your faith.

The story of God's history with humanity is in many ways the story of relationship. It is about God's call to relationship with him and each other. We were created in the image of a relational God: Father, Son and Holy Spirit. Relationships based on the love of God will put others first and make sacrifices for the good of the other.

The coming of Jesus reveals the depth of God's love and his commitment to drawing us to himself in a loving relationship. As we observe the relationship between Jesus and his disciples, and later theirs with each other and the early church, we are given the privilege of peering into the work God wants to do in all of us. I cannot think of a better way to explain this than to follow the discipleship pattern found in the first two chapters of the book of Acts. The following describes what happened in these two chapters and how we might seek to emulate them today.

In Acts 1 and 2 God gives us the astounding story of how the Church began. But he gives us much more than that! God has embedded within these amazing chapters the pattern for how we are to come to faith and then live out our faith as we relate to God, each other, and the world.

---

[a] 2 Timothy 2:2

The story begins with the disciples and others who had followed Jesus gathering in obedience to his command. They waited together in the Upper Room for the Holy Spirit to come upon them and empower them for ministry. They met and prayed together until the day of Pentecost, when God the Father and Jesus Christ the Son honored their obedience by sending the Holy Spirit, who came upon them in tongues of fire and empowered them for ministry.

Immediately the disciples began to proclaim the Gospel. They proclaimed that Jesus Christ was, and is, the promised Messiah. They made it clear that it was the sin of those gathered before them that sent Jesus to the cross. As Peter was speaking to the people, the Holy Spirit convicted them of their sin and their hearts were pierced with the weight of their guilt, and they cried out asking what they should do. This conviction of sin is vital to the proclamation of the Gospel. We see it in Isaiah's cry in the book of Isaiah[a] when he became aware of his profound guilt and the guilt of his people. In deep awareness of the hopelessness of his ability to make himself pure before God he cried out to God. Because of his humble cry, God touched him and forgave his sin. True salvation, admittance into the Kingdom of God, must begin with a humble awareness of our guilt before God and our total inability to save ourselves. As Peter spoke three thousand people did cry out in repentance, received Christ, were baptized, and received the gift of the Holy Spirit.

Those 3,000 people quickly began a lifestyle that was like that of Jesus and his disciples. In deep devotion, they learned as the apostles taught them about Christ and what it meant to know and follow him. They were a people deeply devoted to prayer with each other. They broke bread, shared meals, and partook of the Lord's Supper. They had deep fellowship with each other as they met from house to house.

As described earlier, the Greek word for 'fellowship' is 'koinonia' which means something like an expression of genuine Christianity freely shared among the members of God's family. It is sharing with others, words of encouragement, confessions of failure, statements of need, and the sharing of resources. It is also

---

[a] Isaiah 6:5-6

129

sharing in something with others such as sorrow, joy, or an area of mutual concern. Koinonia is where true godly love seeks the greatest good of the others in an atmosphere where genuine honesty and humility are expressed. It is where Christian brothers and sisters lovingly help restore those who fail rather than judge and reject them. In this atmosphere of true love people can confess their sins and be assured of the forgiveness of God and their friends in Christ. It is a place where people encourage each other in their walk with Christ. It is a life together that is informal and flexible with the focus on spiritually developing God's people rather than routine and structure. This was a lifestyle that happened throughout the week, not just on Sunday morning.[a] The book of First John is a wonderful look at Christian love and the fellowship that naturally flows from it.[b] You will be blessed and challenged by the call God reveals to you through them!

What were the results of this new pattern of life? Signs and wonders were performed by the apostles. We know what some of them were, and I am sure many other amazing things happened. I am sure they saw the miracle of many people coming to faith in Christ. No doubt miracles took place verifying the truth being proclaimed by the apostles. People began to see what they had as gifts from God to be used to help those among them who had a need. This new lifestyle was obviously seen by many who had not yet received Christ and resulted in the fledgling church being viewed with favor among all. What was the result? God added to the church daily those who were being saved! Isn't that our goal?

As God daily adds to the church those who are being saved, it is our responsibility to help them grow to full maturity in Christ.[c] Would not it make sense that God would reveal to us how we are to work in cooperation with him to bring about this result? It seems clear that the pattern revealed in these first two chapters of Acts lays out the foundation for how the church is to fulfill her

---

[a] This is a paraphrase from "Koinonia" by Chuck Swindol
[b] I encourage you to read the entire book of 1 John, especially the following verses: 1:1-7, 2:9-11, 3:10, 3:14-17, 4:7-8, 4:11-12, 4:20-21, and 5:1-2
[c] Ephesians 4:11-16

mission as declared in the Great Commission[a] which results in people living out the Great Commandment[b] as they live transformed lives.

As we gather in small groups it is important that we seek to create an atmosphere that resembles that in Acts 2; an atmosphere that encourages people to grow in their relationship with God and each other. Since many churches have a great heritage in the development and maintaining of Home Groups (called Class Meetings in the early Methodist Church) it is important that we learn from that heritage; that we look to the past to understand what we are to do in the future.

THE FORMAT OF A HOME GROUP

There are several names given to Home Groups, but the objective is still the same as it was in the Methodist Church in the 17th to the early 20th centuries. When I think of a Home Group meeting together, I envision a group of people who desire to grow in their faith, in their love for Christ, and their understanding of how to live out the Christian faith.

Home Groups "foster a community of honesty and personal accountability. The accountability comes not in any prescribed set of rules or confession, but in learning to understand and respond to all of our experiences, good and bad, through the perspective of our relationship with God. I think more about my faith than I ever have in my life, asking myself more and more often, 'How is my life in God?' even outside of the group setting."[19]

In Home Groups people gather to "watch over one another in love" as they "work out their salvation"[c] by encouraging, supporting, and guiding one another on their spiritual journey. This was the goal Paul gave to church leaders when he penned the words above in Ephesians.[d]

The members of a Home Group do not see their Home Group as just a weekly meeting but part of a life together that exists

---

[a] Matthew 28:18-20
[b] Matthew 22:37-40
[c] Philippians 2:12
[d] Ephesians 4:11-16

131

beyond the Home Group meeting. During the week they will be in prayer for one another. Throughout the week they will continue to support and encourage one another in various ways. For example: Phone calls and cards to encourage, share, etc.; two or more meeting together for breakfast or lunch, or sharing an evening meal together. They may care for each other's children so that a couple can have some time alone. Or, a few may gather to help paint a kitchen, or the entire group may gather to build a member's garage and celebrate with a picnic at the end of the day. The entire group, including children, may serve a meal to the homeless or go on a mission trip. The possibilities are endless and all work together, by the power of the Holy Spirit, to help all the members grow in their faith and love for Christ. This is the Christian faith given to us by Christ and passed down to us through the Apostles and the Church Fathers.[a]

Has God laid on your heart someone you can share Christ with? Why not begin by simply inviting them to attend church or a Home Group with you? And consider using this book to share Christ with them, then they will have some tools needed to grow in their faith.

As God tells us through Paul, "Therefore from now on we recognize no one according to the flesh; even though we have known Christ according to the flesh, yet now we know Him in this way no longer. Therefore if anyone is in Christ, he is a new creature; the old things passed away; behold, new things have come. Now all these things are from God, who reconciled us to Himself through Christ and gave us the ministry of reconciliation, namely, that God was in Christ reconciling the world to Himself, not counting their trespasses against them, and He has committed to us the word of reconciliation. Therefore, we are ambassadors for Christ, as though God were making an appeal through us; we beg you on behalf of Christ, be reconciled to God. He made Him who knew no sin to be sin on our behalf, so that we might become the righteousness of God in Him. And

---

[a] The book *Life Together* by Dietrich Bonhoeffer is timeless discussion of Christian fellowship during the Nazi years in Germany.

working together with Him, we also urge you not to receive the grace of God in vain— for He says, "AT THE ACCEPTABLE TIME I LISTENED TO YOU, AND ON THE DAY OF SALVATION I HELPED YOU." Behold, now is "THE ACCEPTABLE TIME," behold, now is "THE DAY OF SALVATION."[a]

---

[a] 2 Corinthians 5:16–6:2

Chapter 13

A Journey of Being Conformed to the Image of Christ
Part One

It is important to be reminded that everything discussed in the previous chapters is not something God forces on us! All of it is an invitation to voluntarily come into a relationship with God and be changed into the image of Christ! Here are a few verses that reveal this truth.

"Just as we have borne the image of the earthy, we will also bear the image of the heavenly."[a]

"and have put on the new self who is being renewed to a true knowledge according to the image of the One who created him."[b]

In the Greek, the word 'image' means, "the image of the Son of God into which true Christians are transformed," *This is the goal of sanctification; to go on the lifelong journey of progressively becoming more like Jesus Christ, inwardly in our character and outwardly in our actions, with the goal of growing in our love for God and people.* The question is, how do we move toward having the image of Christ formed in us? A particularly good statement that sums up the answer is, *God wants to change what we ARE on the inside, and what we DO with our life!*

A revealing verse to help us understand how God molds us into the image of Jesus Christ is found in the book of James which says,

"Even so faith, if it has no works, is dead, being by itself. But someone may well say, 'You have faith and I have works; show me your faith without the works, and I will show you my faith by my works.' You believe that God is one.

---

[a] 1 Corinthians 15:49
[b] Colossians 3:10

You do well; the demons also believe, and shudder. But are you willing to recognize, you foolish fellow, that faith without works is useless?"[a]

The process begins by believing in the truth shared in chapters one through four, accepting Jesus Christ into our life as shared in chapter five, coming to understand that being a Christian is a lifelong journey as shared in chapters six and seven, and beginning to develop the spiritual habits discussed in chapter eight.

When we truly follow this path God slowly conforms us into the image of Christ; *what we ARE on the inside.* The evidence of what we are on the inside is revealed by *what we DO with our life,* which is covered in chapters nine through twelve. These four chapters begin to reveal what we truly are as we: create godly marriages and families, use all the gifts God has given us for his glory, seek God's vision for our life, develop a passion for the lost and share Christ with them, and help others grow in their faith.

In the rest of this chapter, and in the next two chapters, we will take a deeper look at what it means to have the image of Christ formed in our lives and actions, as we serve God in all areas of our lives. In this chapter the focus is on what it means to genuinely love God by exploring the meaning of the Tree of Life and the Tree of the Knowledge of Good and Evil. Then, in the next chapter the focus will be on the inner life of a person with the emphasis on the biblical meaning of Love, Faith, Trust, and Hope. Next, in the following chapter the effects of a person's inner life will be revealed by the way they live a life of Godly wisdom and integrity, as they practice a life of justice and righteousness flowing from the throne of God.

THE TREE OF LIFE AND THE
TREE OF THE KNOWLEDGE OF GOOD AND EVIL

Throughout the Bible God has made it clear that he always wanted us to know, love, and follow him. He desires this because he created us, loved us, and knows what is best for us! This message is revealed right from the beginning of the Bible

---

[a] James 2:17–20

and throughout it! So, lets go on a journey through the Bible to discover this truth by looking at the Tree of Life and the Tree of the Knowledge of Good and Evil.

"Out of the ground the Lord God caused to grow every tree that is pleasing to the sight and good for food; the tree of life was also in the midst of the garden, and the tree of the knowledge of good and evil. ... The Lord God commanded the man, saying, 'From any tree of the garden you may eat freely; but from the tree of the knowledge of good and evil you shall not eat, for in the day that you eat from it you will surely die.'"[a]

"When the woman saw that the tree (of knowledge of good and evil) was good for food, and that it was a delight to the eyes, and that the tree was desirable to make one wise, she took from its fruit and ate; and she gave also to her husband with her, and he ate. Then the eyes of both of them were opened, and they knew that they were naked; and they sewed fig leaves together and made themselves loin coverings. They heard the sound of the Lord God walking in the garden in the cool of the day, and the man and his wife hid themselves from the presence of the Lord God among the trees of the garden. Then the Lord God called to the man, and said to him, '"Where are you?' He said, 'I heard the sound of You in the garden, and I was afraid because I was naked; I hid myself.' And He said, 'Who told you that you were naked? Have you eaten from the tree of which I commanded you not to eat?'"[b]

"Then the Lord God said, 'Behold, the man has become like one of Us, knowing good and evil; and now, he might stretch out his hand, and take also from the tree of life, and eat, and live forever'... So He drove the man out; and at the east of the garden of Eden He stationed the cherubim and the flaming sword which turned every direction to guard the way to the tree of life."[c]

---

[a] Genesis 2:9, 16-17
[b] Genesis 3:6-11
[c] Genesis 3:22, 24

The Tree of Life is mentioned at the beginning of the Bible, the blessings of it are mentioned often throughout the Bible, and it is also at the end of the Bible. It is mentioned first in Genesis, and Adam is not forbidden to eat from it, but it appears he never does. Adam does not need to eat from it because he already has life given by God, who is the center of life. True life is a relationship with God that is a spiritual relationship in the kingdom of God forever. The Tree of Life is God himself in Jesus Christ! With God at the center of our lives we can truly live and enjoy the true freedom he has created us for. In Jesus we have freedom from our sin nature, and instead we have the freedom that comes from the indwelling Holy Spirit of God that comes from surrendering to Jesus Christ, and therefore in response we come to know, love, and follow him throughout our life as we are led by the Holy Spirit. We can have this freedom because on the cross, just before his last breath, Jesus said, "Father, into Your hands I commit My spirit." When this happened the veil of the temple, which represented the separation of humanity from God, was torn from top to bottom. This act of God represented to us the fact that now, because of the death of Jesus Christ, we could now be once again in a relationship with God, who is the Tree of Life!

However, right next to the Tree of Life is the Tree of Knowledge of Good and Evil, and Adam is forbidden to eat from it. To eat from the Tree of the Knowledge of Good and Evil is to make the decision to not live in a loving relationship with God by loving him and obeying his commands. Instead, Adam and Eve reject God and make their own decisions of what is right and wrong. They turn their back on God, who is Life, and the life he had created for them, and walked into darkness, their own version of what is right and wrong. They decided to follow Satan, the liar and deceiver, the very essence of hate and evil.

However, when a choice is made to do this, it is also decided to live outside God's love, protection, guidance, and provision. Without God at the center of our life, there is no true life, only death. And the consequences are deadly to us and the world. Instead of a world living in peace and harmony characterized by self-giving love, the world is marked by self-centeredness which results in deep patterns of sin and evil; people using others to gain something for themselves resulting in broken marriages, broken families, people trapped in cycles of addiction, cycles of revenge and violence, grabs for wealth and power, a war-torn world, and much more. In addition to the sin and evil there is also broken communion with God for eternity, resulting in eternal separation from him.

God, who is the Tree of Life, loves us and wants to give us:

Wisdom: "She (wisdom) is a tree of life to those who take hold of her, and happy (blessed) are all who hold her fast."[a]

Righteousness: "The fruit of the righteous is a tree of life, and he who is wise wins souls."[b]

Fulfillment: "Hope deferred makes the heart sick, but desire fulfilled is a tree of life."[c]

As is a soothing spirit: "A soothing tongue is a tree of life, but perversion in it crushes the spirit."[d]

Lastly, the Tree of Life (God) is clearly seen in the following verses from Revelation,

> "He, who has an ear, let him hear what the Spirit says to the churches. To him who overcomes, I will grant to eat of the tree of life which is in the Paradise of God".[e]

Do you truly hear what this verse says?! All people throughout the world who truly hear in their spirit the Holy Spirit of God and receive Christ and therefore have their sins forgiven and washed away, and follow Christ (the Tree of Life) will be welcome into the Kingdom of God!

> "On either side of the river was the tree of life, bearing twelve kinds of fruit, yielding its fruit every month; and the leaves of the tree were for the healing of the nations. Blessed are those who wash their robes, so that they may have the right to the tree of life and may enter by the gates into the city. ... and if anyone takes away from the words of the book of this prophecy, God will take away his part from the tree of life and from the holy city, which are written in this book."[f]

---

[a] Proverb 3:18
[b] Proverb 11:30
[c] Proverb 13:12
[d] Proverb 15:4
[e] Revelation 2:7
[f] Revelation 22:2, 14, 19

To be in a relationship with God (the Tree of Life) is all about receiving Christ and obeying the great commandment which is,

"Hear, O Israel! The Lord is our God, the Lord is one! You shall <u>love</u> the Lord your God with all your <u>heart</u> and with all your <u>soul</u> and with all your <u>might</u>."[a]

Jesus re-affirmed this commandment from God when he said,

"The foremost is, 'Hear, O Israel! The Lord our God is one Lord; and you shall <u>love</u> the Lord your God with all your <u>heart</u>, and with all your <u>soul</u>, and with all your <u>mind</u>, and with all your <u>strength</u>. The second is this, 'You shall love your neighbor as yourself.' There is no other commandment greater than these."[b]

There are five words in these three verses that reveal to us what is vital to our relationship with God: love, heart, soul, mind, and strength. To understand these words, and apply them to our lives, is to go a long way in understanding why Jesus called them the two greatest commandments. So, let us look at all five.

We must <u>love</u> God

This use of the word 'Love,' in both verses 30 and 31 above, in the Greek language is 'agapao' and means "to welcome, to be fond of, to love dearly"[c]. By using this word, God is inviting us to welcome him into our lives as our Savior and to dearly love him. We know that we are doing this when we love him with all our...

We must love God with all our <u>heart</u>

We must first love God with all our heart, which is 'the center and seat of our spiritual life'. We cannot love him with our soul, mind, and strength without first loving him with all our hearts. Our hearts must be in love with God!

"'For I know the plans that I have for you,' declares the Lord,

---

[a] Deuteronomy 6:4
[b] Mark 12:29-31
[c] The defections of the words: love, heat, soul, mind, and might/strength are from the *Enhanced Strong's Lexicon*

'plans for welfare and not for calamity to give you a future and a hope. 'Then you will call upon Me and come and pray to Me, and I will listen to you. 'You will seek Me and find Me when you search for Me with all your heart.'"[a]

"How blessed are those who observe His testimonies, who seek Him with all their heart."[b]

We must love God with all our *soul*

Next, we must love God with all our soul, 'the seat of the feelings, desires, affections, aversions.' The soul is our will, what we delight in, what we want to do. If we love God with all our heart, we will delight in what he delights in.

"But His delight is in the law of the Lord, and in His law he meditates day and night. He will be like a tree firmly planted by streams of water, which yields its fruit in its season and its leaf does not wither; and in whatever he does, he prospers."[c]

"I cried with all my heart; answer me, O Lord!
I will observe Your statutes.
I cried to You; save me
And I shall keep Your testimonies.
I rise before dawn and cry for help;
I wait for Your words.
My eyes anticipate the night watches,
That I may meditate on Your word.
Hear my voice according to Your lovingkindness;
Revive me, O Lord, according to Your ordinances."[d]

"not by way of eyeservice, as men-pleasers, but as slaves of Christ, doing the will of God from the soul".[e]

In the Greek language soul also means, "the essence which differs from the body and is not dissolved by death."

---

[a] Jeremiah 29:11–13
[b] Psalm 119:2
[c] Psalm 1:2-3
[d] Psalm 119:145-149
[e] Ephesians 6:6

We must love God with all our *mind*

When we love God with all our heart and soul, we will discover with our mind, our 'faculty of understanding, feeling, desiring', the ways of God, and we will love him with all our mind. As you read the following two Scriptures look at the connection between loving God with our minds and the action that follows.

"we are taking every thought captive to the obedience of Christ"[a]

"Only be strong and very courageous; be careful to do according to all the law which Moses My servant commanded you; do not turn from it to the right or to the left, so that you may have success wherever you go. This book of the law shall not depart from your mouth, but you shall meditate on it day and night, so that you may be careful to do according to all that is written in it; for then you will make your way prosperous, and then you will have success. Have I not commanded you? Be strong and courageous! Do not tremble or be dismayed, for the Lord your God is with you wherever you go."[b]

Is not it wonderful that the Lord our God is always near us! He will never leave us or forsake us! The Holy Spirit, who is within us, will always guide us to love God with all our hearts, soul, and mind.

We must obey the will and commands of God with all our *strength*

Strength, our "ability, force, and might" is the actions that flows from what our hearts, souls, and minds desire. To love God with all our heart, soul, and mind, is to do the things God loves with all our strength. Look at these Scriptures that clearly say this.

"Looking about at those who were sitting around Him, He said, 'Behold My mother and My brothers! For whoever does

---

[a] 2 Corinthian 10:5
[b] Joshua 1:7-9

141

the will of God, he is My brother and sister and mother.'"ᵃ

"For you have need of endurance, so that when you have done the will of God, you may receive what was promised."ᵇ

"By this we know that we have come to know Him, if we keep His commandments. The one who says, 'I have come to know Him,' and does not keep His commandments, is a liar, and the truth is not in him; but whoever keeps His word, in him the love of God has truly been perfected. By this we know that we are in Him: the one who says he abides in Him ought himself to walk in the same manner as He walked."ᶜ

"Do not love the world nor the things in the world. If anyone loves the world, the love of the Father is not in him. For all that is in the world, the lust of the flesh and the lust of the eyes and the boastful pride of life, is not from the Father, but is from the world. The world is passing away, and also its lusts; but the one who does the will of God lives forever."ᵈ

"Therefore, since Christ has suffered in the flesh, arm yourselves also with the same purpose, because he who has suffered in the flesh has ceased from sin, so as to live the rest of the time in the flesh no longer for the lusts of men, but for the will of God."ᵉ

Adam and Eve did not love God enough to trust him when he said,

"The Lord God commanded the man, saying, 'From any tree of the   garden you may eat freely; but from the tree of the knowledge of good and evil you shall not eat, for in the day that you eat from it you will surely die'".ᶠ

As a result, they listen to Satan, the liar and deceiver, and turned their back on God, resulting in sin and walking out on God's blessings. They had committed idolatry: the worshiping of false gods.

ᵃ Mark 3:34–35
ᵇ Hebrews 10:36
ᶜ 1 John 2:3–6
ᵈ 1 John 2:15–17
ᵉ 1 Peter 4:1–2
ᶠ Genesis 2:16-17

Psalms 119:161-168 is a good summary of all four loves we are to have for God.

"Princes persecute me without cause,
But my *heart* stands in *awe* of *Your words*.
I *rejoice* at *Your word*,
As one who finds great spoil.
I hate and despise falsehood,
But I *love Your law*.
Seven times a day I *praise* You,
Because of Your *righteous ordinances*.
Those who *love Your law* have great peace,
And nothing causes them to stumble.
I *hope* for Your salvation, O Lord,
And *do Your commandments*.
My *soul keeps Your testimonie*s,
And I *love* them exceedingly.
*I keep Your precept*s and *Your testimonies*,
For all my ways are before You."

Chapter 14

A Journey of Being
Conformed to the Image of Christ
Part Two

As God works in our life to conform us to the image of Christ, there are certain Christlike character traits he desires to mold within us; *what we ARE on the inside*. Among these are: love, faith, trust, and hope, which are covered in this chapter. The first is ...

Love

The goal of living a life of perfect love is about God's ultimate purpose for all his children and is therefore foundational to Christianity. It is found in Matthew which says,

"But I tell you: Love your enemies and pray for those who persecute you, that you may be sons of your Father in heaven. He causes his sun to rise on the evil and the good, and sends rain on the righteous and the unrighteous. If you love those who love you, what reward will you get? Are not even the tax collectors doing that? And if you greet only your brothers, what are you doing more than others? Do not even pagans do that? Be perfect, therefore, as your heavenly Father is perfect."[a]

Throughout the twenty centuries of Christian history perfect love has been described in various ways such as ...

In the 300's St. Augustine said this of love, "What does love look like? It has the hands to help others. It has the feet to hasten to the poor and needy. It has eyes to see misery and want. It has the ears to hear the sighs and sorrows of men. That is what love looks like."[20]

---

[a] Matthew 5:44-48

144

In the 600's a Christian leader by the name of Maximus said this about Jesus' command to love our enemies, "Why did he command this? To free you from hatred, grief, anger, and resentment, and to make you worthy of the supreme gift of perfect love. And you cannot attain such love, if you do not imitate God and love all men equally."[21]

In the 1700's John Wesley had this to say about Jesus' command to love our enemies, "'Love your enemies' see to it that you bear a tender good will to those who are most bitter of spirit against you: who wish you all manner of evil ... 'bless them that curse you' ... 'Do good to them that hate you.' Let your actions show that you are as real in love, as they in hatred..."[22]

Then in the 1900's Donald Grey Barnhouse said, "Love is the key. Joy is love singing. Peace is love resting. Patience is love enduring. Kindness is love's truth. Goodness is love's character. Faithfulness is love's habit. Gentleness is love's self-forgetfulness. Self-control is love being the reins." [23]

Even when we were enemies of God and lost in sin, he still loved us and died on the cross for our salvation; that is true love! When we begin to find ourselves genuinely caring about and feeling genuine godly love toward those who are our 'enemies,' than we will know that God is truly working in our lives. But it is impossible to do this on our own, God's help is needed! That is how Paul loved, and explains how we can love, with God's help, in 1 Corinthians chapters 8-13. The final verse in these chapters is,

> "But now faith, hope, love, abide these three; but the greatest of these is love."[a]

In 1 Corinthians 9 Paul used his liberty from the power of sin, which he received when he accepted Jesus as his Savior through faith. He then grew in his love for God and put all his hope in God. His faith, hope, and love in God led to a deep trust of God, which gave him the strength of God as he obeyed him and spread the gospel of Christ.

In Paul, as in all of us, there is a battle with sin; the desire to do things our own way, rather than obey the will and ways of

---

[a] 1 Corinthians 13:13

God. This is a battle that could only be won in Jesus Christ as Paul writes about in Romans,

> "For we know that the law is spiritual, but I am of the flesh, sold under sin. For I do not understand my own actions. For I do not do what I want, but I do the very thing I hate. Now if I do what I do not want, I agree with the law, that it is good. So now it is no longer I who do it, but sin that dwells within me. For I know that nothing good dwells in me, that is, in my flesh. For I have the desire to do what is right, but not the ability to carry it out. For I do not do the good I want, but the evil I do not want is what I keep on doing. Now if I do what I do not want, it is no longer I who do it, but sin that dwells within me. So I find it to be a law that when I want to do right, evil lies close at hand. For I delight in the law of God, in my inner being, but I see in my members another law waging war against the law of my mind and making me captive to the law of sin that dwells in my members. Wretched man that I am! Who will deliver me from this body of death? Thanks be to God through Jesus Christ our Lord! So then, I myself serve the law of God with my mind, but with my flesh I serve the law of sin."[a]

Verses 9:12, 19 and 22 show the result of winning the battle with sin,

> "but we endure all things so that we will cause no hindrance to the gospel of Christ … For though I am free from all men, I have made myself a slave to all, so that I may win more … To the weak I became weak, that I might win the weak; I have become all things to all men, so that I may by all means save some."

This is the battle Paul speaks of in 1 Corinthians 10. He speaks about our battle with sin, how to overcome it, and how to walk in the Spirit. In love we bring people the good news of salvation in Christ and teach them how to live the life he created us for, to transform us and prepare us for life in heaven. How do we become a people who become like Paul who said, "I have become all things to all men, so that I may by all means save

---

[a] Romans 7:14-25

some.""? How can we follow Jesus' command to follow him, love all people, and be fishers of men? Let us go on a journey through 1 Corinthians 10 to find out.

1 - "For I do not want you to be unaware, brethren, that our fathers were all under the cloud and all passed through the sea;"

Paul is giving a warning here to the believers of Corinth, and to us, to be constantly aware of the forces that can keep us from doing God's will to loving others with his love and winning them to Christ.

The Israelites were on a remarkable journey from slavery to freedom under the guidance of Moses who listened to God and obeyed him. They were going on a journey to the promised land God had prepared for them. But they must listen to and follow Moses to know the way to go. God would protect and lead them as signified by the cloud and destroy all who come to take them back into slavery, as signified by the sea. He was taking them on the journey to a land of freedom as they trusted, loved, and obeyed God.

2 – "and all were baptized into Moses in the cloud and in the sea;"

The people were 'baptized' into a new life just like Moses was. Moses left Egypt as a respected and powerful leader and spent forty years in the desert so he could leave the ways of the world (symbolized by Egypt), and learn how to listen to and trust the voice and ways of God. The desert is symbolic of leaving the ways of our flesh and the ways of the world that entice us to follow them, rather than trusting and following God. When Moses was ready to listen and follow him, God spoke to him through the burning bush and called him to lead the people of Israel to the Promised Land.

Now, the people were to live as a 'baptized' people who followed God's pattern by listening, trusting, and obeying Moses. They too could leave the 'world' (Egypt) and enter the Promised Land and live as a free people of God who could love, listen, trust, and obey God. This is true freedom! This is what it means to be 'baptized' into Moses; they were to follow Moses as he walked through the 'sea' (the ways of the world and our flesh) and follow the 'cloud' (God's way of life that keeps them under his protection). It was to be a journey into a heartfelt love and trust in

God that expressed itself in a delight for the ways of God and living them out in their daily life. This is what God created them, and us, for! So that the world will see God within us and be drawn to him. This is what Nehemiah meant when he wrote,

> "And you divided the sea before them, so that they went through the midst of the sea on dry land, and you cast their pursuers into the depths, as a stone into mighty waters. By a pillar of cloud you led them in the day, and by a pillar of fire in the night to light for them the way in which they should go."[a]

3 - "and all ate the same spiritual food;"

To accomplish this God gave them spiritual food every day, symbolized by the daily supply of manna. All of them had God's teaching through Moses that made it possible to leave behind the old way of life of slavery in Egypt and enter into the life of freedom as loving and obedient children of God in the Promised Land. This truth is seen in these Scriptures,

> "Then the Lord said to Moses, 'Behold, I will rain bread from heaven for you; and the people shall go out and gather a day's portion every day, that I may test them, whether or not they will walk in My instruction.'"[b]

> "He humbled you and let you be hungry, and fed you with manna which you did not know, nor did your fathers know, that He might make you understand that man does not live by bread alone, but man lives by everything that proceeds out of the mouth of the Lord."[c]

> "But He answered and said, 'It is written, 'Man shall not live on bread alone, but on every word that proceeds out of the mouth of God.' "[d]

Spiritual food is the instruction in the ways of God; it gives them, and us, understanding in their mind, and teaches them how to follow the ways of God.

---

[a] Nehemiah 9:11-12 (EVS)
[b] Exodus 16:4 (NAS)
[c] Deuteronomy 8:3 (also see verses 4-19)
[d] Matthew 4:4

4a - "and all drank the same spiritual drink,"

The spiritual drink is the strength and passion God gives to live the new life he is calling them, and us, to live. It is a changed heart that passionately desires to live for God.

> "'Behold, I (the Lord) will stand before you there on the rock at Horeb; and you shall strike the rock, and water will come out of it, that the people may drink.' And Moses did so in the sight of the elders of Israel"[a]

> "You shall remember all the way which the Lord your God has led you in the wilderness these forty years, that He might humble you, testing you, to know what was in your heart, whether you would keep his or not."[b]

The miracle of water coming from a rock was to help them understand, and honestly believe in their hearts, that God was truly with them. He would guide and protect them, and us, if they would keep his commandments!

4b. "for they were drinking from a spiritual rock which followed them; and the rock was Christ."

Christ was there! He was not seen by them, but he was teaching their mind through Moses, and changing their heart through all their experiences, to follow him into the Promised Land. God was, through the nation of Israel, pointing them and the world to the future when Christ would come as the "bread of God." And his name would be called Jesus! And Jesus would lead all who come to him to the true Promised Land when they would never hunger or thirst, as seen through these verses,

> "Jesus then said to them, 'Truly, truly, I say to you, it is not Moses who has given you the bread out of heaven, but it is My Father who gives you the true bread out of heaven. For the bread of God is that which comes down out of heaven, and gives life to the world.' Then they said to Him, 'Lord, always give us this bread.' Jesus said to them, 'I am the bread of life; he who comes to Me will not *hunger*, and he who

---

[a] Exodus 17:6
[b] Deuteronomy 8:2

believes in Me will never *thirst.*'"[a]

"Jesus answered and said to her, 'Everyone who drinks of this water will thirst again, but whoever drinks of the water that I will give him shall never thirst; but the water that I will give him will become in him a well of water springing up to eternal life.'"[b]

"If anyone is thirsty, let him come to Me and drink. He who believes in Me, as the Scripture said, 'From his innermost being will flow rivers of living water.'"[c]

Jesus is the one who provides true spiritual life which lasts forever, true spiritual 'bread' and 'water', as opposed to the 'world' which only seeks to satisfy our lust. As seen in 1 John,

"Do not love the world nor the things in the world. If anyone loves the world, the love of the Father is not in him. For all that is in the world, the lust of the flesh and the lust of the eyes and the boastful pride of life, is not from the Father, but is from the world. The world is passing away, and also its lusts; but the one who does the will of God lives forever."[d]

5 "Nevertheless, with most of them God was not well-pleased; for they were laid low in the wilderness."

God did so much for them! Delivered them from slavery through the ten plagues, parted the Red Sea for them to pass through, and drowned the Egyptian army. He guided them by the cloud, he fed them with manna and water, defended them against their enemies, taught them through Moses, Christ was there with them, etc.!

However, they did not choose to respond by loving God and worshiping him, and by obeying him and his ways of life, even though Moses told them clearly what to do. Therefore, they were clearly without excuse and God did not take pleasure in them, therefore they were punished, and many were killed. And, as we will see, the same message holds true for all people today.

---

[a] John 6:32-35
[b] John 4:13-14
[c] John 7:37-38
[d] 1 John 2:15-17

6 "Now these things happened as examples for us, so that we would not crave evil things as they also craved."

The Israelites were punished by God because they were not living as God had created them to; a life that would bless them and their children. They decided they knew better and received the results of the life they chose. They were punished out of love, so they would decide to choose the ways of God. The love of God corrects us because he knows that we are destroying ourselves, and he knows the best way for us to live. The things that happened to the Israelites are a warning to us! We are not to do as they did! God loves each person and wants all of us to choose his way, the only way, to the Promised Land!

The prodigal son story in the book of Luke[a] is about two sons who are not on the road to living in God's kingdom, the Promised Land. The father, a symbol of God, let them be in rebellion in hopes that they would change their mind and returned to him. When the younger son realized his mistakes and repented, he returned to the father, who welcomes him with open arms of love and forgiveness! The older son, even though he lived in the father's house, did not honor the father for the right reasons. The father begged him to welcome his brother, but his heart was hard and unforgiving, and he refused to really be in the father's kingdom.

God loves us and does not want us to 'crave evil things' like the Israelites did. We are not to be lusting after, longing for, be eager for, things that come from our sinful nature where we choose our own way, rather than God's ways, as said in 1 John,

"Do not love the world nor the things in the world. If anyone loves the world, the love of the Father is not in him. For all that is in the world, the lust of the flesh and the lust of the eyes and the boastful pride of life, is not from the Father, but is from the world. The world is passing away, and also its lusts; but the one who does the will of God lives forever."[b]

So, what did they do that God was not pleased with? How do we avoid their error?

---

[a] Luke 15:11-32

[b] 1 John 2:15-17 (see also Romans 1:24, Ephesians 2:3, 4:22, and 1 Peter 4:2)

7 "Do not be idolaters, as some of them were; as it is written, 'The people sat down to eat and drink, and stood up to play.'"

What was so bad about eating and drinking and playing? To understand why this was evil it is important to look at the context for the saying, which is Exodus 20-32:10. In Exodus 20:1-17 Moses went up on Mount Zion and receive the Ten Commandments from God, and the first one was, "You shall have no other gods before Me." Then in verse 20, "Moses said to the people, 'Do not be afraid; for God has come in order to test you, and in order that the fear of Him may remain with you, so that you may not sin.'"

In Exodus 24:1-4, Moses went back up to Mount Zion to worship and receive instructions for the people. He came down and recounted to the people all the words of the Lord and the ordinances, and all the people answered and said with one voice, "All the words that the Lord has spoken we will do!" Then in 24:4-8 they made a covenant with God and said again,' "All that the Lord has spoken we will do, and we will be obedient!"

Finally, in chapter 32:1-10 the people disobeyed the first of the Ten Commandments by worshiping a Golden Calf. By doing this the people committed idolatry: the worshiping of a false god!

8 "Nor let us act immorally, as some of them did, and twenty-three thousand fell in one day."

This verse comes from a very disturbing event in the book of Numbers which begins by saying,

> "While Israel remained at Shittim, the people began to play the harlot with the daughters of Moab. For they invited the people to the sacrifices of their gods, and the people ate and bowed down to their gods."[a]

The event resulted in the death of twenty-three thousand Israelites!

Immorality often follows on the heels of idolatry. It is defined as: "is to prostitute one's body to the lust of another, to give one's self to unlawful sexual intercourse, to commit fornication, to be given to idolatry, to worship idols, to permit

---

[a] Numbers 25:1-9

one's self to be drawn away by another into idolatry."[a] Idolatry always leads to more sin because, as I said before, to turn your back on God is to decide for yourself what is good or evil, rather than to trust God who is truth and always tells us what is true. Remember what Jesus said when he answered a question from Thomas and answered by saying,

> "I am the way, and the truth, and the life; no one comes to the Father but through Me? ... You say correctly that I am a king. For this I have been born, and for this I have come into the world, to testify to the truth. Everyone who is of the truth hears My voice."[b]

Immorality is deciding that God is not to be trusted! You tell yourself, "God didn't really mean it when he said, 'You shall not commit adultery (idolatrous worship).'"[c]

All sexual activity, except that which is between a married man and woman, is immoral and therefore it is idolatry. The biblical understanding of marriage and family, as a lifelong covenant between one man and one woman and the children that are created from their union, flows from the heart of God. Remember, even before the Fall God created marriage calling Adam and Eve to come together as one when he said,

> "Therefore a man shall leave his father and his mother and hold fast to his wife, and they shall become one flesh"[d]

This definition was reaffirmed by Jesus[e] and by Paul,[f] and in the book of 1 Corinthian when Paul said,

> "Do you not know that your bodies are members of Christ? Shall I then take away the members of Christ and make them members of a prostitute? May it never be! Or do you not know that the one who joins himself to a prostitute is one body with her? For He says, 'The two shall become one flesh.' But the one who joins himself to the Lord is one spirit

---

[a] Enhanced Strong Lexicon
[b] John 14:6, 18:38
[c] Exodus 20:14, see also 1 Thessalonians 4:1-8
[d] Genesis 2:24 ESV
[e] Matthew 19:5
[f] Ephesians 5:31

with Him. Flee immorality. Every other sin that a man commits is outside the body, but the immoral man sins against his own body. Or do you not know that your body is a temple of the Holy Spirit who is in you, whom you have from God, and that you are not your own? For you have been bought with a price: therefore glorify God in your body."[a]

It is important to remember that God, through the people of Israel, was leading humanity to a holy life by loving him, listening to him, trusting him, and obeying him. This begins with being a people who remember to obey the First Commandment which includes "Do not commit adultery."

9 "Nor let us try the Lord, as some of them did, and were destroyed by the serpents."

This event comes from the book of Numbers when the people of Israel complained to Moses and God about how God was caring for them, and reads,

"Then they set out from Mount Hor by the way of the Red Sea, to go around the land of Edom; and the people became impatient because of the journey. The people spoke against God and Moses, 'Why have you brought us up out of Egypt to die in the wilderness? For there is no food and no water, and we loathe this miserable food.'[b]

In response the Lord sent fiery serpents among the people, and they bit the people, so that many Israelites died. So, the people came to Moses and said,

"We have sinned, because we have spoken against the Lord and you; intercede with the Lord, that He may remove the serpents from us.' And Moses interceded for the people. Then the Lord said to Moses, 'Make a fiery serpent, and set it on a standard; and it shall come about, that everyone who is bitten, when he looks at it, he will live.' And Moses made a bronze serpent and set it on the standard; and it came about, that if a serpent bit any man, when he looked to the bronze serpent, he lived."

---

[a] 1 Corinthians 6:15-20 (NAS), See the section on *Making Marriage and Family a Priority* for a deeper look at the importance marriage.
[b] Numbers 21:4-9

If people commit idolatry, they move away from being in a relationship with God and walking in his ways. We lose our trust in him and go from Light into darkness and lose our way in life.[a] We than become fearful and look for someone to blame our problems on, instead of blaming ourselves. That is what the people of Israel did to God; they did not trust him! So, they 'try' God, meaning they question God's character and power. They did not think he had the power and/or the character to care for them. They suffered the consequences of their sin, and many died. They repented and God provided what seemed like a rather peculiar solution to their sin; look at a bronze serpent on a pole and they would be healed!

This event looks backward into the past, and forward into the future. When they remembered their past, as we must do today, we all look to the Garden of Eden and see Adam and Eve listening to the serpent's deception and lies, rather than trusting in the goodness and heart of God. They turned from the Light of God and the way of truth and holy living and follow the serpent (Satan) into the darkness of sin. And the event also looks forward to the future and sees Christ bearing our sin, becoming sin, on the Cross! Remember when Jesus said,

> "Moses lifted up the serpent in the wilderness, even so must the Son of Man be lifted up; so that whoever believes in Him will have eternal life."[b]

In Christ alone there is healing for our sins, and therefore eternal life in the Kingdom of God!

10 "Nor grumble, as some of them did, and were destroyed by the destroyer."

This event of grumbling and its consequences happened in the book of Numbers which in part says,

> "[41] But on the next day all the congregation of the sons of Israel grumbled against Moses and Aaron, saying, 'You are the ones who have caused the death of the Lord's people.' ...
> [44] and the Lord spoke to Moses, saying, [45] 'Get away from among this congregation, that I may consume them

---

[a] see Psalm 119:105
[b] John 3:14-15

instantly.' ... [49] But those who died by the plague were 14,700 ... [7:10] But the Lord said to Moses, 'Put back the rod of Aaron before the testimony to be kept as a sign against the rebels, that you may put an end to their grumblings against Me, so that they will not die.'" [a]

They grumbled which means "to murmur, of those who discontentedly complain," against the leaders God had chosen. They grumbled because they did not like what God provided for them, and they did not want to follow his way of life. Instead, they chose to follow their flesh, which means ultimately to listen to and follow Satan.

God wants to give them, as us, love, and peace, but Satan wants to destroy them because he is "the greatest destroyer of love and peace." They chose not to trust God, and they were destroyed, which means "to put out of the way entirely, abolish, put an end to, ruin."

Remember what the people promised to God before all of this happened in verses 7-10? In Exodus they made a covenant with God and said,

"All that the Lord has spoken we will do and we will be obedient!" [b]

And they were not obedient quite often! It says in verses 6-10 five times, 'some of them did': craved evil things, committed idolatry, were immoral, tried the Lord, and grumbled against God; and they were punished in some way. Why? Because they chose not to trust and obey God, who has shown his love for them by doing so much for them! [c]

11 "Now these things happened to them as an example, and they were written for our instruction, upon whom the ends of the ages have come."

This verse is *especially important*! Some of the words in verse 11 below have after them the Greek meaning of the words and reads, "Now these things happened to them as an example *(of*

---

[a] Numbers 16:41-17:10
[b] Exodus 24:4-8
[c] See Deuteronomy 8:1-10 and Psalm 95 which is a kind of summary of verses 11:5-10.

ruinous events which serve as admonitions or warnings to others), and they were written for our instruction *(admonition, exhortation)*, upon whom the ends of the ages have come *(this is the last age, the consummation of all ages of humanity until Jesus Christ comes again in power and glory to set up God's eternal Kingdom on Earth)*.

God inspired Paul to record these events to warn us, in love, what will happen if we do not heed his warning and do what some of the Israelites did. They craved evil things, were idolatress, practiced immorality, tried the Lord, and grumbled against God instead of loving and obeying God with all their heart, soul, mind, and strength.

The authors of Hebrews and 1 Peter, and other Biblical authors, wrote about this when they said,

"God, after He spoke long ago to the fathers in the prophets in many portions and in many ways, *in these last days* has spoken to us in His Son, whom He appointed heir of all things, through whom also He made the world."[a]

"For He was foreknown before the foundation of the world, but has appeared in *these last times* for the sake of you who through Him are believers in God, who raised Him from the dead and gave Him glory, so that your faith and hope are in God. *Since you have in obedience to the truth purified your souls for a sincere love of the brethren, fervently love one another from the heart*, for you have been born again not of seed which is perishable but imperishable, that is, through the living and enduring word of God."[b]

In these last days how do we love like Paul did? Read James 1:1-15 and then meditate on this song to find the way.

"Trust and Obey" by John Henry Sammis

When we walk with the Lord
In the light of His Word,
What a glory He sheds on our way;
While we do His good will,

---

[a] Hebrews 1:1-2
[b] 1 Peter 1:20-23

He abides with us still,
And with all who will trust and obey.

(Refrain) Trust and obey, for there's no other way
To be happy in Jesus, but to trust and obey.

Not a shadow can rise,
Not a cloud in the skies,
But His smile quickly drives it away;
Not a doubt or a fear,
Not a sigh or a tear,
Can abide while we trust and obey. *(Refrain)*

Not a burden we bear,
Not a sorrow we share,
But our toil He doth richly repay;
Not a grief or a loss,
Not a frown or a cross,
But is blest if we trust and obey. *(Refrain)*

But we never can prove
The delights of His love,
Until all on the altar we lay;
For the favor He shows,
And the joy He bestows,
Are for them who will trust and obey. *(Refrain)*

Then in fellowship sweet
We will sit at His feet,
Or we'll walk by His side in the way;
What says we will do;
Where He sends, we will go,
Never fear, only trust and obey. *(Refrain)*

12 "Therefore let him who thinks he stands take heed that he does not fall."

But how do we love, trust, and obey in such a way that we, in God's love and power and by the Holy Spirit, bring many people to faith in Christ? If we are honest, we often fail at this!

Some of the words in verse 12 have after them the Greek meaning of the words and reads, "Therefore let him who thinks *(to be of opinion, suppose)* he stands *(to be of a steadfast mind)* take heed *(to think they have the ability to discover with their own mind without the guidance of the Holy Spirit)* that he does not fall

158

(to fall under judgment)." Jesus speaks quite often about those who think they hear and understand, but do not, when he says,

> "… because while seeing they do not see, and while hearing they do not hear, nor do they understand." And, of those who do understand when he said, "But blessed are your eyes, because they see; and your ears, because they hear… he who has ears, let him hear."[a]

Therefore, if we are truly seeking to understand what Jesus is saying, we must be people who are humble and fear God's judgment. God calls us to continue to grow in trust and knowledge of Christ, and to love him and believe in him.[b] We must be people who, as Psalm 95:6-8 says,

> "Come, let us worship and bow down,
> let us kneel before the Lord our Maker.
> For He is our God, and we are the people of His pasture
> and the sheep of His hand.
> Today, if you would hear His voice,
> do not harden your hearts"

Because …

13 "No temptation has overtaken you but such as is common to man; and God is faithful, who will not allow you to be tempted beyond what you are able, but with the temptation will provide the way of escape also, so that you will be able to endure it."

This verse is quite clear: there is no temptation in the entire world that is not common to all people. All are tempted! However, the temptation is different for each of us depending on various factors, physical and environmental, that have affected our life and how we react to them. The question is: have we reacted to temptation according to our fallen flesh, or by the guidance of scripture and the power of the Holy Spirit?

Our God is a faithful and loving God, and if we ask humbly, he will guide us out of whatever temptation we are struggling with because he says,

> "For thus says the high and lofty One who inhabits eternity, whose name is Holy: 'I dwell in the high and holy place, and

---

[a] From Matthew 13:10-43 with quotes from Isaiah 6:9-10.
[b] See Romans 11:20, 2 Peter 3:17-18, 1 Peter 1:1-9.

also with him who is of a contrite and humble spirit, to revive the spirit of the humble, and to revive the heart of the contrite.'"[a]

God has, and will always, "provide a way of escape" from temptation so that we can endure it. And the way of escape is found in Scripture which says,

"Make me to know your ways,
O Lord; teach me your paths.
Lead me in your truth and teach me,
for you are the God of my salvation;
for you I wait all the day long. ...
Your word is a lamp to my feet and a light to my path.
I have sworn and I will confirm it,
that I will keep Your righteous ordinances."[b]

When we receive Christ as our Savior, it is important to understand that the rest of our life is a journey of making him our Lord, which means loving him with all our heart, soul, mind, and strength, as explained in verses 5-11 above. As each of us live our life in the spiritual darkness of the fallen world there is only one 'Light' who can guide our feet so that we will not stumble and fall. To stumble and fall is to give into our fallen flesh and Satan's temptation, and not follow the ways of God. The deception of mans 'wisdom' and the subtle ways it can creep into our lives are deep and numerous and plays on the weakness of our sin nature. Therefore, on our journey through life, it is important to hold up the Light, who is Jesus Christ, who will guide us daily throughout our life. That Light is the scriptures God has given us, and the guidance of the Living Word, Jesus Christ, as he guides us by the Holy Spirit in the context of life in the Church. This is how God provides the way of escape so that all of us will be able to endure temptation! Therefore, the Daily Prayers of the Church have in their confession these words,

"For the sake of your Son Jesus Christ, have mercy on us and forgive us; that we may delight in your will, and walk in your ways, to the glory of your name. Amen. ... May Almighty

---

[a] Isaiah 57:15 ESV
[b] Psalm 25:4-5 (NAS) and Psalm 119:105-106

God have mercy on us, forgive us our sins, through Jesus Christ our Lord, and strengthen us to live in the power of the Holy Spirit, all our days. Amen."

Because this is true, it is important to ...

14-15 "Therefore, my beloved, flee from idolatry. I speak as to wise men; you judge what I say."

Flee to Jesus! Seek safety in Jesus from the danger of all our sinful patterns and all temptations that flow over us when we commit idolatry (see verse seven above)! He is the *only* one who can empower us to walk on the narrow path that leads to holiness and to heaven! Jesus means it when he says in the book of Matthew,

> "Enter through the narrow gate; for the gate is wide and the way is broad that leads to destruction, and there are many who enter through it. For the gate is small and the way is narrow that leads to life, and there are few who find it."[a]

How do we flee to Jesus and walk on his path!?

First, be a wise person, one who is knowledgeable in the ways of God. Honestly believe what John says,

> "We know that no one who is born of God sins; but he who was born of God keeps him, and the evil one does not touch him. We know that we are of God, and that the whole world lies in the power of the evil one. And we know that the Son of God has come and has given us understanding so that we may know Him who is true; and we are in Him who is true, in His Son Jesus Christ. This is the true God and eternal life"[b].

And secondly, be like "Little children, guard yourselves from idols."[c]

The person who takes seriously all that is said in verses 1-15 and applies it to their life, this is the person who judges wisely all that is said by God through Paul, and that takes seriously the spiritual wisdom that follows in the next verse.

---

[a] Matthew 7:13-14 (NAS)
[b] 1 John 5:18-20
[c] 1 John 5:21, see 2 Kings 22:14-23:3

16-17 "Is not the cup of blessing which we bless a sharing in the blood of Christ? Is not the bread which we break a sharing in the body of Christ? Since there is one bread, we who are many are one body; for we all partake of the one bread."

Christ shed his blood on the cross for our forgiveness, and allowed the breaking of his body for us, so all people could be in fellowship with him. As the people of God share in Holy Communion and see the cup and bread blessed, we give praise and honor to Christ for the benefit his people have received because of his sacrifice.

The sharing of the cup and bread remind us again and again what Christ did for his followers so that we could be in fellowship with him and be in the same kind of fellowship with one another. When the people of God begin to understand how deep the love of God is for us, we want to do the same for him by loving him with all our heart, soul, mind, and strength, and to love one another with the same love Christ has for us.

And since Christ has *one* body represented by the *one* loaf of bread, all of us are to be *one* body in such a profound way that we are truly *one* in Christ and *one* with each other. And in response all of us are to share the love of Christ with those who are not Christians; so, they can see the love of Christ in us and come to faith in him. This is one of the messages receive from sharing in Holy Communion. And another one of the reasons his people partake in Holy Communion is to suffer for Christ in the same way he suffered for us; by dying to self and seeking to "delight in his will, and walk in his ways, to the glory of God's name."

When Christians are truly sharing in Holy Communion we are partaking in and proclaiming the Lord's death until he comes again.[a]. Therefore, in ...

31b-33 ... whatever you do, do all to the glory of God. Give no offense either to Jews or to Greeks or to the church of God; just as I also please all men in all things, not seeking my own profit but the profit of the many, so that they may be saved.

When we say that we do all things to the glory of God, the word "glory" means the one who has, "the kingly majesty which belongs to him as supreme ruler, majesty in the sense of the

---

[a] 1 Corinthians 11:26

absolute perfection of the deity." All that his people do is for him and him alone, for he is God and worthy of all glory and honor, therefore we forget about ourselves and can only do what will glorify God!

This means that we have the humility of Christ and speak the truth in love so that others see the love of Christ in us. It does not matter who we are talking too; an agnostic, those of another religion, a friend, or an enemy. You get the idea! The only goal is to have them think about and hopefully accept the truth of who Christ is, and what he has done for them.

It is important not to offend others in such a way that causes them to reject the truth that the Holy Spirit has been seeking to present to them. It is imperative to be led by the Holy Spirit! This must be done in a spirit of love and humility as we present the claims of the gospel to them, like Jesus did to the woman at the well in the book of John.[a] And, at the same time listening to their beliefs and opinions, and seeking to discover Christian truth within them that we can use to lead them to Christ, and at the same time not to approve what they believe that we do not agree with. Again, we do not do this to please ourselves, or to gain anything for ourselves. It is done for one purpose only; to honor God by having them come to faith in Christ, and being a part of the Kingdom of God, all to God's glory! This is true love! Love that is overflowing with "joy, peace, patience, kindness, goodness, faithfulness, gentleness, and self-control."[b]

1 Corinthians chapters 8-13, which teaches about true love, begins with "but love edifies," and ends with this beautiful verse, "But now faith, hope, love; abide these three; with the greatest of these is love." In this true love Paul saw the harvest Jesus talks about when he said in the book of Matthew,

> "And Jesus went throughout all the cities and villages, teaching in their synagogues and proclaiming the gospel of the kingdom and healing every disease and every affliction. When he saw the crowds, he had compassion for them, because they were harassed and helpless, like sheep without a shepherd. Then he said to his disciples, 'The harvest is

---

[a] John 4:1-42
[b] Galatians 5:22-23

plentiful, but the laborers are few; therefore pray earnestly to the Lord of the harvest to send out laborers into his harvest.'"[a]

All around him Paul saw the harvest Jesus talked about, people without a shepherd, and in the power and love of Jesus, he gave up all to bring the gospel of Christ to them! God is calling us to be those who do the same!

The Father, Son, and Holy Spirit, who in a mystery no one can possibly understand are One God, is the one true God who calls us to love him with all our heart, soul, mind, and strength. He calls us to demonstrate this love in faith, as we abide in him by following the example of Jesus Christ throughout our life, in sure and certain hope that he will guide us to our eternal home in paradise! The book of Colossians sums up the love and attitude God desires for us to have toward our families, friends, coworkers, neighbors, church family, strangers we meet, enemies, in fact all people!

"Therefore, if you have been raised up with Christ, keep seeking the things above, where Christ is, seated at the right hand of God. Set your mind on the things above, not on the things that are on earth. For you have died and your life is hidden with Christ in God. When Christ, who is our life, is revealed, then you also will be revealed with him in glory. Therefore, consider the members of your earthly body as dead to immorality, impurity, passion, evil desire, and greed, which amounts to idolatry. For it is because of these things that the wrath of God will come upon the sons of disobedience, and in them you also once walked, when you were living in them. But now you also, put them all aside: anger, wrath, malice, slander, and abusive speech from your mouth. Do not lie to one another, since you laid aside the old self with its evil practices, and have put on the new self who is being renewed to a true knowledge according to the image of the One who created him— a renewal in which there is no distinction between Greek and Jew, circumcised and uncircumcised, barbarian, Scythian, slave and freeman, but

---

[a] Matthew 9:35–38

Christ is all, and in all.

So, as those who have been chosen of God, holy and beloved, put on a heart of compassion, kindness, humility, gentleness and patience; bearing with one another, and forgiving each other, whoever has a complaint against anyone; just as the Lord forgave you, so also should you. Beyond all these things put on love, which is the perfect bond of unity. Let the peace of Christ rule in your hearts, to which indeed you were called in one body; and be thankful. Let the word of Christ richly dwell within you, with all wisdom teaching and admonishing one another with psalms and hymns and spiritual songs, singing with thankfulness in your hearts to God. Whatever you do in word or deed, do all in the name of the Lord Jesus, giving thanks through him to God the Father." [a]

As we seek to love God, and others with God's love, let us be a people who are astounded at what God has prepared for us![b]

"Things which eye has not seen and ear has not heard,
And which have not entered the heart of man,
All that God has prepared for those who love Him."
1 Corinthians 2:9.

Faith and Trust

If we consistently follow the spiritual disciplines, which God has given to us, we will grow in our love for him in our hearts, souls, and minds, resulting in a growing of faith and trust in him. Faith in God, which is a gift from him, is a conviction that God truly created and loves us, and teaches the truth through the Bible, especially in the birth, life, teaching, Crucifixion, Resurrection, and Ascension of Jesus Christ. This faith increases our trust in God, and a conviction that he can be relied on in every area and event of our life, as he conforms us to the image of Christ.

---

[a] Colossians 3:1–17, see also Romans 13:8-14. Read Matthew 26:36-46 and ask yourself; am I loving like Jesus did, or like the disciples?
[b] Listen to a message on Christian love, "The Radical Nature of Christianity" by Pastor Jim Cymbala of The Brooklyn Tabernacle on their YouTube channel.

In the Bible 'faith' and 'trust' are often used together to convey the truth that true faith results in trust. The word 'faith' can be translated as 'assurance' or 'pledge' depending on which word best conveys the message of the verse it is used in, as these and many other verses show.

"Now faith is the assurance of things hoped for, the conviction of things not seen."[a]

"let us draw near with a sincere heart in full assurance of faith, having our hearts sprinkled clean from an evil conscience and our bodies washed with pure water."[b] "And we desire that each one of you show the same diligence so as to realize the full assurance of hope until the end,"[c]

And the word 'trust' can be translated as 'confidence' or 'reliance' depending on which word best conveys the message of the verse it is used in, as these few verses show.

"This was in accordance with the eternal purpose which He carried out in Christ Jesus our Lord, in whom we have boldness and confident access through faith in Him."[d]

"Therefore let us draw near with confidence to the throne of grace, so that we may receive mercy and find grace to help in time of need."[e]

"Therefore, do not throw away your confidence, which has a great reward. For you have need of endurance, so that when you have done the will of God, you may receive what was promised."[f]

"Now, little children, abide in Him, so that when He appears, we may have confidence and not shrink away from Him in shame at His coming. If you know that He is righteous, you know that everyone also who practices righteousness is born of Him.". ... "Beloved, if our heart does not condemn us, we have confidence before God; and whatever we ask we

---

[a] Hebrews 11:1
[b] Hebrews 10:22
[c] Hebrews 6:11
[d] Ephesians 3:11–12
[e] Hebrews 4:16
[f] Hebrews 10:35–39

receive from Him, because we keep His commandments and do the things that are pleasing in His sight." [a]

Hope

As a person grows in their belief of the true God as revealed in the Bible and accepts the invitation of God to go on the incredible journey of knowing, loving, and following Jesus Christ, he or she will grow in their love of God, and in their faith and trust in him. This growing faith will increase into a deep trust in the hope God gives for this life and for eternity!

The word 'hope' in the Bible means: "expectation of good, joyful and confident expectation of eternal salvation and God who is its foundation." All people want to have hope in their life; hope for a good and peaceful life that has godly purpose for themselves, their family and friends, their careers, that they can be used by God to make the world a better place, and for God's help in these and other areas of life. As God's children follow his teaching as found in the Bible, they can have his help in all areas of life, but as we know things do not always go the way we expect them to go. Does this mean God does not care, or he does not have the power to help us? The Bible tells us just the opposite! God does care for us deeply, loves us, and he is all powerful! We can be assured that God will bring good in every area of life as we have faith, trust in him, and follow him. But there is one area of life we have no control over and must depend completely on God: our salvation and eternal life in heaven! We must have a faith, which is a gift from God, that gives us the assurance and conviction that he, through Jesus Christ has given us the gift of salvation and eternal life in heaven! The following is a glimpse of what the Bible says about hope.

"Now faith is the assurance of things hoped for, the conviction of things not seen." [b]

"For in hope we have been saved, but hope that is seen is not hope; for who hopes for what he already sees? But if we hope for what we do not see, with perseverance we wait eagerly

---

[a] 1 John 2:28–29, 1 John 3:21–24

[b] Hebrews 11:1

for it."[a]

"For He was foreknown before the foundation of the world, but has appeared in these last times for the sake of you who through Him are believers in God, who raised Him from the dead and gave Him glory, so that your faith and hope are in God."[b]

"the ground upon which hope is based, which is Christ in you, the hope of glory."[c]

"For we through the Spirit, by faith, are waiting for the hope of righteousness."[d]

"He saved us, not on the basis of deeds which we have done in righteousness, but according to His mercy, by the washing of regeneration and renewing by the Holy Spirit, whom He poured out upon us richly through Jesus Christ our Savior, so that being justified by His grace we would be made heirs according to the hope of eternal life."[e]

A great summary of love, faith, trust, and hope is that they are inseparable from each other; faith, trust, and hope in God cannot exist without a true and abiding love for God. These Christlike character traits are what God desires to mold within us; *what we ARE on the inside. God wants to change what we ARE on the inside, so that we can DO what he created us for.*

And what are we to do with these internal character traits? If they are real, they must exhibit themselves in godly wisdom and integrity as we follow Jesus Christ in all areas of our live as we practice justice and righteousness.

---

[a] Romans 8:24–25
[b] 1 Peter 1:20–21
[c] Colossians 1:27
[d] Galatians 5:5
[e] Titus 3:5–7

Chapter 15

A Journey of Being Conformed to the Image of Christ
Part Three

What are we to DO with our life? Life as God intended it to be is a long journey, a good journey, and ultimately the only journey worth taking, for only this journey results in true wisdom and integrity, and pleases God as seen in this Scripture,

> "Who may ascend the hill of the Lord? Who may stand in his holy place? He who has clean hands and a pure heart..."[a]

Wisdom and Integrity

It is difficult to say in a few words what it means to be a person of wisdom and integrity. Wisdom is essentially to be a person who puts into action the truths revealed in the word of God. Jesus says in Matthew,

> "Therefore everyone who hears these words of Mine and acts on them, may be compared to a wise man who built his house on the rock."[b]

Wise people are those who steep themselves in the word of God, so they can make wise decisions in every area of life. They honestly believe what it says in these verses in Proverbs and Psalm,

> "Acquire wisdom! Acquire understanding! Do not forget nor turn away from the words of my mouth."[c]

> "So teach us to number our days, that we may present to You a heart of wisdom."[d]

---

[a] Psalm 24:3-4
[b] Matthew 7:24
[c] Proverb 4:5
[d] Psalm 90:12

Wisdom should lead to integrity. Integrity is to finish well in the race marked out for us, to be a person who is the same on the inside as on the outside. They live in active fellowship, receiving the encouragement and accountability that they need from others who are in the same race, and share the same goal of finishing well. It is the journey that takes us through life and leads us to be a person of integrity.

Being a person of wisdom and integrity is to live the well-balanced life we have been discussing. It is walking throughout life in God's Truth, which is Jesus Christ as he is revealed in scripture, with his people, and not walking in the ways and deception of the world, as declared in Psalm 26.

> "Vindicate me, O Lord, for I have walked in my integrity,
> And I have trusted in the Lord without wavering.
> Examine me, O Lord, and try me;
> Test my mind and my heart.
> For Your lovingkindness is before my eyes,
> And I have walked in Your truth.
> I do not sit with deceitful men,
> Nor will I go with pretenders.
> I hate the assembly of evildoers,
> And I will not sit with the wicked.
> I shall wash my hands in innocence,
> And I will go about Your altar, O Lord,
> That I may proclaim with the voice of thanksgiving
> And declare all Your wonders.
> O Lord, I love the habitation of Your house
> And the place where Your glory dwells.
> Do not take my soul away along with sinners,
> Nor my life with men of bloodshed,
> In whose hands is a wicked scheme,
> And whose right hand is full of bribes.
> But as for me, I shall walk in my integrity;
> Redeem me, and be gracious to me.
> My foot stands on a level place;
> In the congregations I shall bless the Lord."

Justice and Righteousness

All that has been said in this and the previous two chapters must result in a life of justice and righteousness, which are the very foundation of the throne of God, as seen in these Scriptures.

"Thus says the LORD: 'Let not the wise man boast in his wisdom, let not the mighty man boast in his might, let not the rich man boast in his riches, but let him who boasts boast in this, that he understands and knows me, that I am the LORD who practices steadfast love, justice, and righteousness in the earth. For in these things I delight,' declares the LORD."[a]

"You have a strong arm; Your hand is mighty, Your right hand is exalted. Righteousness and justice are the foundation of Your throne; Lovingkindness and truth go before You."[b]

"Righteousness will go before him and will make his footsteps into a way."[c]

"Therefore be imitators of God, as beloved children; and walk in love, just as Christ also loved you and gave Himself up for us, an offering and a sacrifice to God as a fragrant aroma."[d]

'Justice' in the Hebrew language means the creating of just laws according to the ways of God that are enforced in the culture. This kind of justice punishes those who are violating the ways and commandments of God and protects those who are victims of injustice. 'Righteousness' in the Hebrew language stands for each person being ethically right according to the ways of God in their heart, soul, and mind, and the actions that flow from them. The scriptures above, and many more throughout the Bible, are important to every person and the culture itself.

Justice and righteousness are linked together in the verses above and other scriptures, and together they form the very foundation of the throne of God; they are the foundation of the moral universe God created. When they are ignored and therefore not practiced chaos reigns in the world. When they are understood

---

[a] Jeremiah 9:23-24
[b] Psalm 89:13–14
[c] Psalm 85:13
[d] Ephesians 5:1–2 (NAS)

171

and practiced the presence of God, the Light of Christ, shatters chaos and darkness, resulting in peace, order, and stability reigning in the culture. All that has been said in this book is ultimately about living a life that is based on having the kind of relationships God created us for; a relationship with him through faith in Christ and purposefully growing in that relationship. That growth is evident when a person conducts all relationships with people with godly love, fairness, generosity, and equity.

In the verses above God declares that he, "practices steadfast love, justice, and righteousness in the earth," a justice and righteousness that are the foundation of his throne. Out of his deep love God has revealed how he created us to live. His revelation comes as he speaks to us daily through prayer as he guides us by the Holy Spirit, the Bible, and the Church, as we walk into the world in the footsteps, he provides for us in the life of his Son Jesus Christ.

God is always doing this so that we can have peace in our lives and in the world, rather than the darkness and chaos we see so often. As each one of us seeks to live our lives according to the ways of God, we are helping create a godly order in our lives, families, community, nation, and the world. This is practicing justice and righteousness as God works through us, day by day, to create a world of perfect love.

What if a growing number of people would humbly pray and surrender to God so that he could shape us into the people he created us to be on the inside, so that we can do what he created us for in the world? Where do we start?

➤ First, each one of us must daily humbly bow before God and pray for ourselves! We must praise and thank God for who he is, praise him for our salvation, seek his forgiveness daily for our sins, and ask for his wisdom and strength for the day.

➤ Next, we must pray for God's Church. Pray that he would send into his church Pastors and Priests of deep biblical faith to be its leaders. And that all Christians would faithfully follow Christ by proclaiming salvation in Christ alone to the people they know and discipling them until they are mature in the faith. Then, they too can be in ministry to all the people they know so that they may know Christ.

➤ It is important also to pray for ours and all marriages and families. These are created by God to be the foundation of a moral culture, a place for the most intimate relationships, and the discipleship of children.

➤ Prayer also gives us the opportunity to bring before the Lord the needs of those who are are suffering in some way, and those in any kind of trouble. God always listens to our prayers for others and answers in love according to his wisdom for that person.

➤ Most certainly we must pray for our nation and all in authority in business, entertainment, education, journalism, politics, and government. Pray that God would raise up people who love him and his ways, people who make decisions in humility, and have a desire to honor God and serve others with no thought of themselves.

This is just a few areas to pray for, obviously there are more. What a difference your prayers can make in the world for God's glory as his justice and righteousness reigns in the world! Then, at the end of our life all of us could have the goal of saying with Paul,

"I have fought the good fight, I have finished the race, I have kept the faith. Now there is in store for me the crown of righteousness, which the Lord, the righteous Judge, will award to me on that day."[a]

Heavenly Father, in you we live and move and have our being: We humbly pray you so to guide and govern us by your Holy Spirit, that in all the cares and occupations of our life we may not forget you, but may remember that we are ever walking in your sight; through Jesus Christ our Lord. Amen.[b]

---

[a] 2 Timothy 4:7-8 (NIV)
[b] From the Book of Common Prayer

Chapter 16

A Journey of a Living a Blessed Life as Seen in Ephesians

Throughout this book we have explored what it means to live a blessed life as God intended when he created us. We began by briefly exploring *The God of Scripture* and *Our Rejection of God,* and then moved into *Our Attempts to Reach God,* and next came to understand that *With God There is No Compromise.* Then, in *The Only Path to the True God* and *Stepping onto the Path of Following Jesus* the amazing truth that God has provided a path which is found only in the Son of God, who is Christ Jesus!

Then, in the next two chapters we discovered that we not only need to come into faith in Christ for our salvation, but that we must also go on the lifelong journey of growing in our love for Jesus Christ and what it means to follow him. In the next eight chapters we discussed the habits, priorities, and virtues God enables us to live as citizens of the Kingdom of God. This is what makes us 'fit for heaven!'

I invite you to explore the journey God invites you to go on by studying the book of Ephesians. This book does a great job declaring what God has done for us, how we are to live as a result of what God has done, and what we must do to stay on the journey God has created us for; the life Jesus called us to when he said, "For the gate is small and the way is narrow that leads to life, and there are few who find it".[a] On the next page read each one of the three sections of Ephesians, meditate on it, and then write your answers to the questions that are asked. Take your time to do this study; it is a beautiful message of love from God because he wants us to receive all he has created us for!

---

[a] Matthew 7:13-14

A Journey of a Living a Blessed Life as Seen in Ephesians

Your Identity as a Child of God - Ephesians 1–3

The first three chapters do a great job of declaring what *God has done out of love for you,* and what you must do to *receive* what you *do not deserve!* In Ephesians 1:3 it says, "Blessed be the God and Father of our Lord Jesus Christ, who has blessed us with every spiritual blessing in the heavenly places in Christ." Look for and write down all the ways that God has blessed you, and what you must do to receive them. For a clue look in 1:13, 2:1-7.

Your Heart and Actions as a Follower of Jesus
Ephesians 4-6:9

In the next two and a half chapters you discover how you are to *walk through life in love and gratitude*, because of what God has done for you. Look for and write down all the ways God has called you to, "walk in a manner worthy of the calling with which you have been called" in every area of your life.

Your Strength as you Follow Jesus - Ephesians 6:10-24

In the last section you will discover what God calls you to do that keeps you on the journey God has created you for. Look for and write down who is *not* your enemy, and who *is* your real enemy in verses 6:10-12 (also see Revelation 12:17 where our enemy is called a 'dragon'). Then, discover how you can, with God's wisdom, ways, help, and power, to *stand strong* in your fight against him in verses 13-24.

Because all of this is true all of us must call out to God and say,
"I cried with all my heart; answer me, O Lord!
I will observe Your statutes.
I cried to You; save me and I shall keep Your testimonies.
I rise before dawn and cry for help; I wait for Your words.
My eyes anticipate the night watches,
that I may meditate on Your word.
Hear my voice according to Your lovingkindness;
Revive me, O Lord, according to Your ordinances.
Those who follow after wickedness draw near;
they are far from Your law.
You are near, O Lord, and all Your commandments are truth.
Of old I have known from Your testimonies
that You have founded them forever." Psalm 119:145–152

Chapter 17

Holy Communion:
The Journey in Sacrament

Now, let us look at what it means to go on the journey of knowing, loving, and following Jesus, by taking a brief look at the second sacrament Jesus gave to us, Holy Communion, also called The Lord's Supper or The Eucharist.

The Passover

Just before his Crucifixion Jesus celebrated the Passover with his disciples. The Passover feast was a continuous reminder to Israel that they were enslaved by the Egyptians and powerless to free themselves. They had cried out to God to free them, and God heard their cry for deliverance from slavery. Through Moses and the ten plagues they saw that God had not forgotten them, that he cared deeply for them, and that he had a plan for them. Because he loved and cared for them, God came against and defeated the overwhelming power that enslaved them, culminating in their deliverance through the parted waters of the Red Sea, and the destruction of the Egyptian army in the sea. The Israelites understandably had a great celebration after they had crossed through the sea and saw the destruction of the Egyptian Army.

The yearly Passover meal was a celebration of all God had done to free them, with the focus on the last plague when the Angel of Death killed the firstborn of the Egyptians but passed over the homes of the Israelites because they had placed the blood of an innocent lamb over the doorposts of their homes.[a]

However, it soon became apparent that God had remembered them not only to deliver them from slavery; he had also delivered them to shape them into a people who would love, trust, and obey him, and to send them on a mission that would bless the entire

---

[a] See Exodus 12:3-5, Exodus 15:1-21, Leviticus 23:12, Hebrews 9:14, 1 Peter 1:19

176

world. Throughout the books of Exodus through Deuteronomy God revealed to the people of Israel that they were his treasured possession *and* that in response they would listen to him and obey him. Doing so, they would be a "kingdom of priests and a holy people ... so that my name may be proclaimed in all the earth." This meant they would be a nation through whom God would reveal himself to the rest of the world. Therefore, their lives individually, and as a community, would be lived in such a way that the world would be drawn to God and blessed by becoming his people.[a]

Passover Continues Today in Holy Communion

The last Passover meal occurred when Jesus celebrated it with his disciples the day before he was crucified. What occurred at that meal is highly symbolic and has profound significance in helping us understand the deeper meaning of the life, death, Resurrection, and Ascension of Jesus, and the impact it is to have on our individual lives and the life of the Church. The message of the Passover continues today through Holy Communion and has the same purpose in the Church today. We understand the story of the Jewish people as a foretelling, or a prediction, of the purpose of the Church. Because this is true, we must not receive Holy Communion lightly! It is given to us by Jesus Christ himself to continually remember what God has done for us, and as a response what we are to do for God as we forget ourselves and live for his glory![b]

As we celebrate Holy Communion, we must first remember that we are helpless to overcome the power of sin in our lives. But God has not forgotten us! He loves us deeply and has come to rescue us from the bondage and guilt of sin and eternal death. God rescued us by sending his son Jesus who opened the door to paradise where he now sits at the right hand of his Father.[c] We receive the gift of salvation when we humbly come to God seeking his forgiveness, and he responds by forgiving us,

---

[a] See Genesis 12:3, 22:18, 26:4, 28:14, Exodus 9:13-16, 19:3-6, Deuteronomy 4:20, 6:1-2, 4-5, 10:12-13, Acts 3:25, Galatians 3:8
[b] See 1 Corinthians 11:23-34
[c] See chapters four and five to review who Jesus is and how he opened the door to paradise.

delivering us from the power of sin and eternal death, and receiving us as his child.[a]

As we are reminded of how Jesus went through the denials and betrayals before his death, we are to remember that we also have often denied and betrayed him by not following him.[b] We have not forgiven others as he forgave us[c], and are in deep need of his continuing forgiveness. Therefore, before we take Holy Communion, we pause to confess our sins and hear the good news that we are forgiven. This is cause for celebration and worship!

During Holy Communion we are reminded that at the last Passover meal with his disciples Jesus took some bread and after blessing it, he broke it and gave it to the disciples saying, "Take, eat; this is My body." Then, when he had taken the cup and given thanks he gave it to them saying, "Drink from it, all of you; for this is My blood of the covenant, which is poured out for many for forgiveness of sins."[d] Their sins would now be 'passed over!' Jesus then said, "do this in remembrance of me,"[e] making it a sacrament.

Holy Communion is a calling and commitment, in response to all that Jesus Christ has done for us, to live as Spirit empowered followers of Christ. As people who use the life of Christ as our model for how to live as Christians, we seek to draw others to Christ as we fulfill the Great Commandment and Great Commission given to us by Jesus himself.[f]

We might think of Holy Communion as a summary of the great story of the People of God, and what it means to be a follower of Jesus Christ who is anxiously waiting for his return. It is a ritual that enacts what lies at the very heart of the Christian faith. It continuously reminds us of what it means to make our baptism a reality on our journey through life as followers of Jesus Christ, as we proclaim Christ to the world.

---

[a] See Ephesians 1:7, Colossians 3:13, 1 John 1:9, 2:12

[b] See Matthew chapters 5-7, 25 and the first two pages of chapter 14 as summaries of what it means to be a follower of Jesus Christ.

[c] See Matthew 6:12-15, 18:21-35, Mark 11:26, Colossians 3:12-15, Ephesians 4:32 to read about forgiving others.

[d] Matthew 26:26-28, also see Mark 14:22-24 and Luke 22:19-20

[e] Luke 22:19, 1 Corinthians 11:24-25

[f] Matthew 22:34-40, Matthew 28:18-20

Chapter 18

The Beginning of the Real Journey

Finally, the day will come when our journey in this life is over. On that day, whether we die a natural death or the Lord returns at his final coming at the end of the age, Jesus Christ will welcome all who have humbly bowed and received him as Savior and followed him as Lord, into paradise. In preparation for that Day, please read Matthew 13, 24-25, Mark 13, and 2 Peters 3 that speak about the return of Christ at the end of the age and how to prepare for his glorious return. *Please be sure you are ready!*

When Christ welcomes us into paradise we will be <u>*glorified*</u> (saved from the presence of sin) and live forever in the presence of God in the perfect world that he will create. Jesus tells us of this wonderful future he has for those who receive, love, and follow him, in verses such as the following:

"Now the dwelling of God is with men, and he will live with them. They will be his people, and God himself will be with them and be their God. He will wipe every tear from their eyes. There will be no more death or mourning or crying or pain, for the old order of things has passed away."[a]

"Do not store up for yourselves treasures on earth, where moth and rust destroy, and where thieves break in and steal. But store up for yourselves treasures in heaven, where moth and rust do not destroy, and where thieves do not break in and steal. For where your treasure is, there your heart will be also."[b]

"'Do not let your hearts be troubled. Trust in God; trust also in me. In my Father's house are many rooms; if it were not so, I would have told you. I am going there to prepare a place

---

[a] Revelation 21:3-4 (NIV)
[b] Matthew 6:19-21

179

for you. And if I go and prepare a place for you, I will come back and take you to be with me that you also may be where I am. You know the way to the place where I am going.

Thomas said to him, 'Lord, we don't know where you are going, so how can we know the way?'

Jesus answered, 'I am the way and the truth and the life. No one comes to the Father except through me.'"[a]

"Dear friends, now we are children of God, and what we will be has not yet been made known. But we know that when he appears, we shall be like him, for we shall see him as he is. Everyone who has this hope in him purifies himself, just as he is pure."[b]

Knowing, loving, and following Jesus Christ is a great journey, but it is not an easy journey. However, it is the one you were created for! Hebrews 11 speaks of many of the heroes of the faith who, even though the journey was long and often difficult, persevered on the path through the life God had for them. They did not think they would receive all of God's blessings in this life, but because they knew God was good and trustworthy, in faith they looked forward to the astounding rewards God was preparing for them and all who persevere in following Christ. We see their vision and passion in verses like these,

"Now faith is being sure of what we hope for and certain of what we do not see. ... And without faith it is impossible to please God, because anyone who comes to him must believe that he exists and that he rewards those who earnestly seek him. ... All these people were still living by faith when they died. They did not receive the things promised; they only saw them and welcomed them from a distance. And they admitted that they were aliens and strangers on earth. ... Instead, they were longing for a better country—a heavenly one. Therefore God is not ashamed to be called their God, for he has prepared a city for them."[c]

"I saw the Holy City, the new Jerusalem, coming down out

---

[a] John 14:1-6
[b] 1 John 3:2-3
[c] Hebrews 11:1, 6, 13, 16

of heaven from God, prepared as a bride beautifully dressed for her husband."[a]

May God put in each of us the same faith, vision, and passion for the heavenly country they had! As we wait for that wonderful day let us do what Jude, most likely Jesus' half-brother, tells us.

"But you, beloved, ought to remember the words that were spoken beforehand by the apostles of our Lord Jesus Christ, that they were saying to you, 'In the last time there will be mockers, following after their own ungodly lusts.' These are the ones who cause divisions, worldly-minded, devoid of the Spirit. But you, beloved, building yourselves up on your most holy faith, praying in the Holy Spirit, keep yourselves in the love of God, waiting anxiously for the mercy of our Lord Jesus Christ to eternal life. And have mercy on some, who are doubting; save others, snatching them out of the fire; and on some have mercy with fear, hating even the garment polluted by the flesh. Now to Him who is able to keep you from stumbling, and to make you stand in the presence of His glory blameless with great joy, to the only God our Savior, through Jesus Christ our Lord, be glory, majesty, dominion and authority, before all time and now and forever. Amen." [b]

Let us end with the last chorus from Georg Friedrich Händel "Messiah" which is:

Worthy is the Lamb that was slain, and hath redeemed us to God by His blood, to receive power, and riches, and wisdom, and strength, and honour, and glory, and blessing.
Blessing and honour, glory and power, be unto Him that sitteth upon the throne, and unto the Lamb, for ever and ever. Amen.[c]

---

[a] Revelation 21:2
[b] Jude 17–25 (NAS)
[c] Revelation 5:12-14

Conclusion

Thank you for taking the time to read "An Invitation to The Incredible Journey of Knowing, Loving, and Following Jesus Christ". I appreciate your taking the journey, and I hope you were blessed by God as you read it. In closing, I would like to share one experience I had in ministry that I think sums up a lot of what I have said in this book. A few years ago, I was a director for a summer church camp for elementary children. One evening we decided to take a night hike on a winding trail in the woods with about seventy children and their counselors. With flashlights in their hands, we began our journey through the woods and down the winding trail. I was the last one in a line of campers and their counselors. As I looked ahead of me all I could see in the dark was the winding trail of light from the flashlights and hear the laughter of children.

At that moment I thought of Psalm 119:105 which says, "Your word is a lamp to my feet and a light to my path." I thought, "What if those children didn't have flashlights? They would be tripping and falling, and they would not be laughing! That is a great picture of the Christian life! If we have Jesus, who is the Word of God, guiding us by the Holy Spirit on our journey through life we could stay on the path God has for us and avoid many tears."

Jesus is the Light that guides us along the path that leads to eternal life in paradise! Jesus is the Truth that daily shows us how to walk safely on the path of life God created us for! Therefore, as Psalm 43:3 declares, our prayer should always be,

> "O send out Your light and Your truth, let them lead me; let them bring me to Your holy hill and to Your dwelling places."[a]

---

[a] See John 1:1-5, 8:12, 12:46 which speaks of Jesus as our Light and John 1:14, 14:6, 18:37 which tells us that Jesus is The Truth.

Conclusion

To me this reveals that the Christian life is much more than a set of beliefs. It is a transformed life as we follow Jesus Christ by living a life as declared and revealed in the Bible, as we worship in the church with the fellowship of believer, as we are led by the Holy Spirit, and as we serve in the church and the world, all to the glory of the Father!

In this book I have barely begun to describe the incredible journey God calls us to go on. So please continue to pursue and follow Jesus Christ with all your heart, soul, mind, and strength!

I hope your heart has found rest in Christ because, as St. Augustine said, "You have made us for yourself, O Lord, and our heart is restless until it rests in you." (From St. Augustines "Confessions")

I hope your journey with God will continue to be strengthened as you daily turn to God and pray, "Search me, O God and know my heart; try me and know my anxious thoughts; and see if there be any hurtful way in me, and lead me in the everlasting way"[a], so you can, "Trust in the LORD with all your heart and do not lean on your own understanding. In all your ways acknowledge Him, and He will make your paths straight."[b]

And may, "Almighty God, who after the creation of the world didst rest from all thy works and sanctify a day of rest for all thy creatures: Grant that we, putting away all earthly anxieties, may be duly prepared for the service of thy sanctuary, and that our rest here upon earth may be a preparation for the eternal rest promised to thy people in heaven; through Jesus Christ our Lord. Amen." (A Collect for Saturdays from "The Book of Common Prayer")

May your journey continue throughout your life until you see Jesus Christ face to face and spend eternity with all the Church in the new world God will create. With the Apostle Paul, I pray for all of us,

"For this reason I bow my knees before the Father, from whom every family in heaven and on earth derives its name,

---

[a] Psalm 139:23-24
[b] Proverbs 3:5–6

that he would grant you, according to the riches of His glory, to be strengthened with power through His Spirit in the inner man, so that Christ may dwell in your hearts through faith; and that you, being rooted and grounded in love, may be able to comprehend with all the saints what is the breadth and length and height and depth, and to know the love of Christ which surpasses knowledge, that you may be filled up to all the fullness of God. Now to Him who is able to do far more abundantly beyond all that we ask or think, according to the power that works within us, to Him be the glory in the church and in Christ Jesus to all generations forever and ever. Amen."[a]

Let us continue in our journey through life remembering to give "Glory to the Father, and to the Son, and to the Holy Spirit: as it was in the beginning, is now, and will be forever." We must do it in love, faith, and trust in God, because he loves us and has done so much for us. As we follow Jesus remember that he is the Prince of Peace who is *always* with us in every circumstance of life.[b] He is calling us, the Church, to respond by going on the incredible journey of knowing, loving, and following Jesus Christ!

The Song of the Redeemed
Revelation 15:3-4

O ruler of the universe, Lord God,
great deeds are they that you have done,
surpassing human understanding.
Your ways are ways of righteousness and truth,
O King of all the ages.

Who can fail to do you homage, Lord,
and sing the praises of your Name?
for you only are the Holy One.
All nations will draw near and fall down before you,
because your just and holy works have been revealed.

---

[a] Ephesians 3:14–21
[b] Philippians 4:4-9

Appendix

Recommended Books, YouTube channels, and Movies for continuing your journey

Invitation to a Journey: A Road Map for Spiritual Formation by M. Robert Mulholland Jr.

The Deeper Journey: The Spirituality of Discovering Your True Self by M. Robert Mulholland Jr.

Shaped By the Word by M. Robert Mulholland Jr.

The Imitation of Christ and *On the Passion of Christ* by Thomas à Kempis

Mere Christianity by C.S. Lewis

The Benedict Option and *How Dante Can Save Your Life* by Rod Dreher

Listening to the Bible: The Art of Faithful Biblical Interpretation by Christopher Brian

Kingdom People by James B. Scott & Molly Davis Scott

Life Together by Dietrich Bonhoeffer

Knowing God by J. I. Packer

The Workbook on the Seven Deadly Sins by Maxie Dunnam & Kimberly Dunnam Reisman

The Epic of Eden by Sandra L. Richter

Please visit my blog at: knowlovefollowjesus.blogspot.com/

There are many great teachings on these YouTube channels: Seedbed, Heart Cry, Crazy Love, The Brooklyn Tabernacle with Pastor Jim Cymbala, and Focus on the Family.

Mother Teresa in a 2003 movie by Ignatius Press that tells of the amazing story of nun called by God to care for the extremely poor of Calcutta and around the world.

Nobel is a movie by Word Entertainment LLC, A Warner/Curb Company. It is an amazing story of how God called an Irish woman to build orphanages in Vietnam.

Amazing Grace is a 2006 Bristol Bay Productions LLC, 2007 Twentieth Century Fox. It is a powerful movie about how William Wilberforce, a member of the British Parliament, was called by God to abolish the slave trade and slavery in the British Empire.

End of the Spear is a 2005 movie by Every Tribe Entertainment about missionaries who evangelized the people of the tropical rain forest of eastern Ecuador.

185

Morning Prayer from My Daily Office

Morning and Evening Prayer had used in public and private setting for centuries and when it is used daily, or are often as possible, it provides a structured way of doing daily prayer and provides a daily reading of Psalms, Old Testament, New Testament, and the Gospel.

"My Daily Office is an abbreviated and customizable version of the Daily Office used by Christians around the world. My Daily Office provides liturgy for a personal time of morning and evening prayer derived from the Daily Office found in the Book of Common Prayer." (My Daily Office is written and maintained by Jim LaGrone, Manna Software, LLC, Wilmore, Kentucky.)

Morning Prayer

OPENING VERSE

Briefly meditate on the following to prepare your heart for morning prayer.

Oh send out thy light and thy truth; let them lead me, let them bring me to thy holy hill and to thy dwelling!   —Psalm 43:3

CONFESSION OF SIN

Take a few moments to pray to confess your sins and acknowledge your need for God's grace and forgiveness.

Most merciful God, we confess that we have sinned against you in thought, word, and deed, by what we have done, and by what we have left undone. We have not loved you with our whole heart; we have not loved our neighbors as ourselves. We are truly sorry and we humbly repent. For the sake of your Son Jesus Christ, have mercy on us and forgive us; that we may delight in your will, and walk in your ways, to the glory of your name. Amen.

End by acknowledging God's mercy and realizing that He has forgiven your sins in Christ Jesus.

May Almighty God have mercy on us, forgive us our sins, through Jesus Christ our Lord, and strengthen us to live in the power of the Holy Spirit, all our days. Amen

THE INVITATORY
Move to a time of praise by praying the Invitatory and then the Gloria.

O Lord, open our lips and our mouth shall proclaim your praise.

Glory to the Father, and to the Son, and to the Holy Spirit: as it was in the beginning, is now, and will be forever. Amen.

Alleluia!

THE PSALM
Read one or more of the Psalms.
(A few months of reading are on the pages after My Daily Prayer)

THE READING
At this time, you may read one or more additional readings from the Old Testament, New Testament, and the Gospels.
(A few months of reading are on the pages after My Daily Prayer)

THE APOSTLES' CREED or THE NICENE CREED
Recite the Apostles' Creed, or the Nicene Creed, acknowledging the universal truths of the Christian faith.

THE APOSTLES' CREED
I believe in God, the Father Almighty,
maker of heaven and earth;

And in Jesus Christ his only Son our Lord;
who was conceived by the Holy Spirit,
born of the Virgin Mary,
suffered under Pontius Pilate,
was crucified, dead, and buried;
He descended into hell.
The third day he rose again from the dead.
He ascended into heaven,
and sitteth on the right hand of God the Father almighty.
From thence he shall come to judge the quick and the dead.

I believe in the Holy Spirit,
the holy catholic Church,
the communion of saints,
the forgiveness of sins,
the resurrection of the body,
and the life everlasting. Amen.

THE NICENE CREED

We believe in one God,
the Father, the Almighty,
maker of heaven and earth,
of all that is, seen and unseen.

We believe in one Lord, Jesus Christ,
the only Son of God,
eternally begotten of the Father,
God from God, light from light,
true God from true God,
begotten, not made,
of one Being with the Father;
through him all things were made.
For us and for our salvation
he came down from heaven,
was incarnate of the Holy Spirit and the Virgin Mary
and became truly human.
For our sake he was crucified under Pontius Pilate;
he suffered death and was buried.

On the third day he rose again in accordance with the Scriptures;
he ascended into heaven
and is seated at the right hand of the Father.
He will come again in glory to judge the living and the dead,
and his kingdom will have no end.

We believe in the Holy Spirit, the Lord, the giver of life,
who proceeds from the Father and the Son,
who with the Father and the Son is worshiped and glorified,
who has spoken through the prophets.
We believe in one holy catholic and apostolic Church.
We acknowledge one baptism for the forgiveness of sins.
We look for the resurrection of the dead,
and the life of the world to come.
Amen.

THE LORD'S PRAYER

Pray The Lord's Prayer, taking your time and meditating on each line as you pray.

Our Father, who art in heaven,
hallowed be thy name,
thy kingdom come,
thy will be done,
on earth as it is in heaven.
Give us this day our daily bread.
And forgive us our trespasses,
as we forgive those who trespass against us.
And lead us not into temptation,
but deliver us from evil.
For thine is the kingdom,
and the power,
and the glory, forever.
Amen.

THE INTERCESSION

Use the following intercessory prayer to help you focus on specific concerns.

Show us your mercy, O Lord; And grant us your salvation. Clothe your ministers with righteousness; Let your people sing with joy. Give peace, O Lord, in all the world; For only in you can we live in safety. Lord, keep this nation under your care; And guide us in the way of justice and truth. Let your way be known upon earth; Your saving health among all nations. Let not the needy, O Lord, be forgotten; Nor the hope of the poor be taken away. Create in us clean hearts, O God; And sustain us with your Holy Spirit.

Take some time to pray for yourself and others. Let the Spirit lead you and guide you as you pray.

• The Universal Church, its members, and its mission
• The Nation and all in authority
• The welfare of the world
• The concerns of the local community
• Those who suffer and those in any trouble

THE COLLECT
Pray the following collect.

Morning Collect for Peace

O God, the author of peace and lover of concord, to know you is eternal life and to serve you is perfect freedom: Defend us, your humble servants, in all assaults of our enemies; that we, surely trusting in your defense, may not fear the power of any adversaries; through the might of Jesus Christ our Lord. Amen.

BENEDICTION
Conclude with the following benediction.

Glory to God whose power, working in us, can do infinitely more than we can ask or imagine: Glory to him from generation to generation in the Church, and in Christ Jesus for ever and ever. Amen.

—Ephesians 3:20, 21

Below are a few days of readings for My Daily Office to get you started as you use My Daily Office. The Christians year begins four Sundays before Christmas, on the Sunday falling on or nearest to November 30, and focuses on preparation for the coming of Christ on Christmas. There are three cycles of readings which last one year each, and then repeat.

Daily Readings for Year A

Go to:
https://lectionary.library.vanderbilt.edu/daily.php?year=A
for the rest of year A, and then substitute B or C for A in the address above for years 2 or 3.

Year A

Thursday (beginning, November 28, 2019) Psalm 122; Daniel 9:15-19; James 4:1-10

Friday - Psalm 122; Genesis 6:1-10; Hebrews 11:1-7

Saturday - Psalm 122; Genesis 6:11-22; Matthew 24:1-22

Sunday - First Sunday of Advent Isaiah 2:1-5; Psalm 122; Romans 13:11-14; Matthew 24:36-44

Monday - Psalm 124; Genesis 8:1-19; Romans 6:1-11

Tuesday - Psalm 124; Genesis 9:1-17; Hebrews 11:32-40

Wednesday - Psalm 124; Isaiah 54:1-10; Matthew 24:23-35

Thursday - Psalm 72:1-7, 18-19; Isaiah 4:2-6; Acts 1:12-17, 21-26

HISTORICAL PRAYERS

The peace of our Lord Jesus Christ be with you and with all men in all places who have been called by God and through Him, through whom is glory. Amen. - St. Clement of Rome (1st Century)

O Lamb of God, who takes away the sin of the world, look upon us and have mercy upon us; you who are yourself both victim and priest, yourself both reward and redeemer, keep safe from all evil those whom thou hast redeemed, O Savior of the world. Amen.
St. Irenaeus (130-202)

O Lord, who has mercy upon all, take away from me my sins, and mercifully kindle in me the fire of thy Holy Spirit. Take away from me the heart of stone, and give me a heart of flesh, a heart to love and adore thee, a heart to delight in thee, to follow and to enjoy thee, for Christ's sake. Amen. - St. Ambrose of Milan (339-397)

O good shepherd, seek me out, and bring me home to your fold again. Deal favorably with me according to thy good pleasure, till I may dwell in your house all the days of my life, and praise you forever and ever with them that are there. Amen.
St. Jerome (342-420)

Lord, you have given us your Word for a light to shine upon our path; grant us so to meditate on that Word, and to follow its teaching, that we may find in it the light that shines more and more until the perfect day; through Jesus Christ our Lord. Amen.
St. Jerome (342-420)

Almighty God, who has given us at this time with one accord to make our common prayer to you; and does promise that when two or three are gathered together in your name you will grant their request: fulfill now, O Lord, the desires and petitions of your servants, as may be most expedient for them; granting us in this world knowledge of thy truth; and in the world to come life everlasting. Amen.
St. Chrysostom (347–407)

Lord Jesus, let me know myself and know You,
and desire nothing save only You.
Let me hate myself and love You.
Let me do everything for the sake of You.
Let me humble myself and exalt You.
Let me think of nothing except You.
Let me die to myself and live in You.

Let me accept whatever happens as from You.
Let me banish self and follow You,and ever desire to follow You.
Let me fly from myself and take refuge in You,
That I may deserve to be defended by You.
Let me fear for myself.
Let me fear You, and let me be among those who are chosen by You.
Let me distrust myself and put my trust in You.
Let me be willing to obey for the sake of You.
Let me cling to nothing save only to You,
And let me be poor because of You.
Look upon me, that I may love You..
Call me that I may see You,
and for ever enjoy You. Amen. - St. Augustine (354-430)

Christ with me, Christ before me,
Christ behind me, Christ in me,
Christ beneath me, Christ above me,
Christ on my right, Christ on my left,
Christ when I lie down, Christ when I sit, Christ when I stand,
Christ in the heart of everyone who thinks of me,
Christ in the mouth of everyone who speaks of me,
Christ in every eye that sees me,
Christ in every ear that hears me. Amen. - St. Patrick (387-493)

Gracious and holy Father, give me wisdom to perceive you,
intelligence to fathom you, patience to wait for you, eyes to behold
you, a heart to meditate upon you, and a life to proclaim you,
through the power of the Spirit of Jesus Christ our Lord. Amen.

St. Benedict (480-547)

Alone with none but you, my God, I journey on my way. What need
I fear, when you are near O king of night and day? More safe am I
within your hand than if a host did round me stand. Amen.

St. Columba (521-597)

Leave me alone with God as much as may be. As the tide draws the
waters close in upon the shore, make me an island, set apart, alone
with you, God, holy to you. Then with the turning of the tide prepare
me to carry your presence to the busy world beyond, the world that
rushes in on me till the waters come again and fold me back to you.
Amen. - St. Aidan (Died 651)

Now let me praise the keeper of Heaven's kingdom, the might of the
Creator, and his thought, the work of the Father of glory, how each

of wonders the Eternal Lord established in the beginning. He first created for the sons of men Heaven as a roof, the holy Creator, then Middle-earth the keeper of mankind, the Eternal Lord, afterwards made, the earth for men, the Almighty Lord. Amen.

St. Caedman (658-680)

Lord, because you have made me, I owe you the whole of my love; because you have redeemed me, I owe you the whole of myself; because you have promised so much, I owe you my whole being. Moreover, I owe you as much more love than myself as you are greater than I, for whom you gave yourself and to whom you promised yourself. I pray you, Lord, make me taste by love what I taste by knowledge; let me know by love what I know by understanding. I owe you more than my whole self, but I have no more, and by myself I cannot render the whole of it to you. Draw me to you, Lord, in the fullness of your love. I am wholly yours by creation; make me all yours, too, in love. Amen.

St. Anselm (1033-1109)

Lord, make me an instrument of thy peace.
Where there is hatred, let me sow love;
Where there is injury, pardon;
Where there is doubt, faith;
Where there is despair, hope;
Where there is darkness, light;
Where there is sadness, joy.
O Divine Master, grant that I may not so much seek
To be consoled as to console,
To be understood as to understand,
To be loved as to love;
For it is in giving that we receive;
It is in pardoning that we are pardoned;
It is in dying to self that we are born to eternal life. Amen.

St. Francis of Assisi (1181-1226)

I beg you, Lord, let the fiery, gentle power of your love take possession of my soul, and snatch it away from everything under heaven, that I may die for love of your love as you saw fit to die for love of mine. Amen. - St. Francis of Assisi (1181-1226)

Grant me, O Lord my God, a mind to know you, a heart to seek you, wisdom to find you, conduct pleasing to you, faithful perseverance in waiting for you, and a hope of finally embracing you. Amen.

St. Thomas Aquinas (1225-1274)

Lord, You know what is best; let this be done or that be done as You please. Give what You will, as much as You will, when You will. Do with me as You know best, as will most please You, and will be for Your greater honor. Place me where You will and deal with me freely in all things. I am in Your hand; turn me about whichever way You will. Behold, I am Your servant, ready to obey in all things. Not for myself do I desire to live, but for You—would that I could do this worthily and perfectly! Amen. - St. Thomas À Kempis (1380-1470)

Take, O Lord, and receive all my liberty, my memory, my understanding, and my whole will. You have given me all that I am and all that I possess: I surrender it all to you that you may dispose of it according to your will. Give me only your love and your grace; with these I will be rich enough, and will have no more to desire. Glory be to the Father, and to the Son, and to the Holy Spirit. As it was in the beginning, is now, and ever shall be, world without end. Amen. - St. Ignatius Loyola (1491-1556)

Christ has no body now but yours,
No hands, no feet on earth but yours,
Yours are the eyes through which he looks
Compassion on this world,
Yours are the feet with which he walks to do good,
Yours are the hands, with which he blesses all the world.
Yours are the hands, yours are the feet,
Yours are the eyes, you are his body.
Christ has no body now but yours. - St. Teresa of Avila (1515-1582)

Lord, I am no longer my own, but Yours. Put me to what You will, rank me with whom You will. Put me to doing, put me to suffering. Let me be employed for You or laid aside for You, exalted for You or brought low for You. Let me be full, let me be empty. Let me have all things, let me have nothing. I freely and heartily yield all things to Your pleasure and disposal. And now, O glorious and blessed God, Father, Son, and Holy Spirit, You are mine, and I am Yours. So be it. And the covenant which I have made on earth, let it be ratified in heaven. Amen. - John Wesley (1703-1791)

Bibliography

[1] Thomas à Kempis, *Imitation of Christ,* (Ignatius Press, San Francisco 2005) p. 11

[2] Dietrich Bonhoeffer, *Creation and Fall*, (Toucstone, New York, NY 1997) p 73

[3] C.L. Lewis, *Mere Christianity*, (Collier Books, Macmillan Publishing Company 1952) p. 110-111

[4] Dietrich Bonhoeffer, *Creation and Fall*, (Toucstone, New York, NY 1997) p 73

[5] Dietrich Bonhoeffer, *God is in The Manger*, (Westminster John Knox Press, 2010)

[6] Miroslav Volf, *Exclusion and Embrace,* (Abington Press, Nashville, TN 1996) p. 298

[7] Saint Augustine, *The Trinity*, (New City Press, Hyde Park, New York) p. 153

[8] Thomas à Kempis, *Imitation of Christ,* (Ignatius Press, San Francisco 2005) Book III.19

[9] John Wesley, *The Works of John Wesley, Sermons Vols. 1-2,* (Baker Books, Grand Rapids, Michigan) p. 3

[10] A. W. Tozer, *Man: The Dwelling Place of God,* (The Alliance Witness) Chapter 10

[11] John Wesley, *The Works of John Wesley, Journal Vols. 1-2,* (Baker Books, Grand Rapids, Michigan) p. 103

[12] Dietrich Bonhoeffer, *Creation and Fall / Temptation,* (Touchtone, New York, NY) p. 131-142

[13] Thomas à Kempis, *On the Passion of Christ,* (Ignatius Press, San Francisco 2004) p. 52

[14] Dietrich Bonhoeffer, *Psalms: The Prayer Book of the Bible,* (Augsburg, Minneapolis, MN) p. 64

[15] John Wesley, *The Works of John Wesley, Sermons Vols. 1-2,* (Baker Books, Grand Rapids, Michigan) p 3

[16] Robert Mulholland Jr., *Shaped By The Word,* (Upper Room Books, Nashville, TN) p. 151

[17] George Müller, *Answers to Prayer from George Müller's Narratives,* (Bookworm at bookworm.librivox@gmail.com)

[18] International Leadership Institute, *Christian to the Core,* (ILI Team Publishing, iliteam.org/christiantothecore) p. 5

[19] Kevin Watson, *The Class Meeting,* (Seedbed Publishing, Franklin, TN) p. 14

[20] Augustine of Hippo, *Confessions*, (Moody Press, Chicago)

[21] Maximus the Confessor, azquotes.com/author/28502-

[22] John Wesley, *Catholic Spirit, The Works of John Wesley, Journal Vols. 1-2*, (Baker Books, Grand Rapids, Michigan) p. 492

[23] Donald Grey Barnhouse, sermoncentral.com